God's Ground Force

BARBARA SULLIVAN

God's Ground Force

BARBARA SULLIVAN

BETHANYHOUSE
Minneapolis, Minnesota

God's Ground Force
Copyright © 2006
Barbara Sullivan

Cover design by Eric Walljasper

Italics within quoted Scripture represents emphasis by the author.

Unless otherwise identified, Scripture quotations are from the HOLY BIBLE, NEW INTERNATIONAL VERSION®. Copyright © 1973, 1978, 1984 by International Bible Society. Used by permission of Zondervan Publishing House. All rights reserved.

Scripture quotations identified KJV are from the King James Version of the Bible.

Scripture quotations identified AMP are from the Amplified Bible. Old Testament copyright © 1965, 1987 by the Zondervan Corporation. The Amplified New Testament copyright © 1958, 1987 by the Lockman Foundation. Used by permission.

Scripture quotations identified The Message are from *The Message*. Copyright © 1993, 1994, 1995 by Eugene H. Peterson. Used by permission of NavPress Publishing Group.

Scripture quotations identified TLB are from *The Living Bible* © 1971 owned by assignment by Illinois Regional Bank N.A. (as trustee). Used by permission of Tyndale House Publishers, Inc., Wheaton, IL 60189. All rights reserved.

Published by Bethany House Publishers
11400 Hampshire Avenue South
Bloomington, Minnesota 55438

Bethany House Publishers is a division of
Baker Publishing Group, Grand Rapids, Michigan.

Printed in the United States of America

ISBN-13:   978-0-7642-0138-7
ISBN-10:   0-7642-0138-7

Library of Congress Cataloging-in-Publication Data

CIP data applied for

ISBN 0-7642-0138-7

This book is dedicated to

the selfless volunteers—the ground forces—

of Spirit of God Fellowship,

Harvey House,

and Tabitha House.

Acknowledgments

To my husband, John, whose vision has birthed our many ministries, thanks for all your support, comments, and suggestions. This book is filled with your wisdom and life.

To my son, Tom, for taking time to read the pages and give me your ideas. Thanks also for your chapter on Kids Church and your much-needed help in editing my poems.

To Jeanne Hedrick, for doing a very thoughtful and inspired editing job. Your comments made the book much better. Thank you also for your many prayers and words of encouragement.

To the intercessors of Spirit of God Fellowship, who prayed me through the tough parts, the waiting times, and the discouragement, and brought me to the finish line.

To Kent Garborg, a great friend, who believed in this project and knocked on doors until it became a reality. Thanks, Kent.

To Tim Peterson, Brett Benson, and Dan Olson, the marketing team, who gave me a day of their valuable time and enormous encouragement at a low time in my life.

To Kyle Duncan, for giving me the opportunity to share our journey with other members of the body of Christ. Thank you also for your commitment to excellence in Christian publishing.

To Bethany House Publishers: You are passionate about the right things in Christian publishing. May you continue to be blessed in all your endeavors.

Contents

Introduction

*In his heart a man plans his course, but the
Lord determines his steps.*

PROVERBS 16:9

I am eternally grateful that God does not show us
all at once the blueprint for our lives. Oh, He has a plan all right.
But we can't see it a lot of the time. Instead, we stumble along,
one day at a time, trying desperately to follow Jesus. Sometimes
we rush ahead of Him and wonder why the "way" seems so tough.
I thought His yoke was easy! Other times we lag far behind. Those
are the boring, unfulfilled periods of life. *Where is the abundant life
He promised?*

Then there are the detours we choose. *I've prayed and I just
know this is His will for me!* Only when we reach the dead ends do
we realize our mistake. Our growth level determines whether we
will quickly return to the right path, breathing a silent and grateful
prayer, or slink back slowly, dragging our feet, still questioning. *I
know that was God's will for me, but. . . .*

Still, in some incomprehensible way, God's grace and predes-
tination mingle together to get us where we are supposed to be
when we are supposed to be there. God unfailingly works out His
plan for our lives.

I'm so glad it works like that. Otherwise, I would have missed many incredible surprises. I would have assessed my gifts and talents and planned my life accordingly. By my appraisal, I am totally unqualified to do everything I have done or am presently engaged in doing!

I am also thankful that I was not called to make this journey by myself. My husband of forty-five years, and a committed group of believers who began meeting in our home in 1972, accompanied me. As my husband, John, loves to say, "We didn't know where we were going, but we knew there was more to life than we were experiencing."

God took a small group of white, middle-class suburbanites, with no ministry or Bible training, and birthed through us thirty ministries among the inner-city African-American and Hispanic population. He blessed us with a Christian grammar school of 400 students, a day-care facility of 200, a multipurpose church building, a youth center, homes for men and women ex-substance abusers, two resale facilities, and a boxing club and art center for inner-city youth.

Every so often it hits me: *How did all this happen?* I cannot logically explain it, but I do know that during this journey we learned some things about God. For one thing, we learned that "real religion, the kind that passes muster before God the Father, is this: Reach out to the homeless and loveless in their plight, and guard against corruption from the godless world" (James 1:27 THE MESSAGE).

Today we hear a lot about the fivefold ministry to equip the saints—and rightly so. The church will work more efficiently when each of us discovers our gift. However, in this search we often mistake the means for the end. The knowledge we receive through study materials, tapes, and conferences is "to prepare God's people for *works of service,* so that the body of Christ may be built up" (Ephesians 4:12).

Many Christian churches today have wonderful programs for those within their hallowed walls, but the poor and destitute won't enter because they don't have the right clothes or are not sure they would even be welcomed. We need to be reminded that we aren't called to wait till they come to us; God always sends us out to find them! Our congregation has learned through experience that when we go out to serve those forgotten people in society, they are drawn in by the love of God, working through us.

Perhaps this is why George Barna wrote, "After nearly two decades of studying Christian churches in America, I'm convinced that the typical church as we know it today has a rapidly expiring shelf life."[1] He goes on to discuss the frenzy of religious activity to produce more programs, buildings, and conferences, but concludes that we are losing people faster than any other major institution in the nation.

Why?

I believe it has something to do with our modern-day view of spirituality. Instead of God and the Bible being the center of our faith, belief now revolves around the individual's needs. What we need becomes the primary reason for God's existence. And in our attempts to be "seeker friendly" we have sometimes avoided mentioning some portions of the Bible lest we offend somebody. After all, if large numbers of people stop coming, our success as a church is threatened.

But maybe we have listened to the wrong voices. Can numbers, buildings, and programs measure spiritual success? Or is there a subtle nuance that we are missing in our calculation? Paul Tournier in his book *The Adventure of Living*, defines success in a different way.

> God has a purpose: the entire Bible proclaims this. What matters is that His plan (involving us) should be understood and fulfilled. So, in the light of the Bible, the problem is shifted onto new ground. The question is no longer whether one is succeeding or failing, but whether one is fulfilling God's purpose or not, whether one is adventuring with Him or against Him.
>
> It is, of course, always a joyful thing to succeed. But the joy is very deceptive if it comes from the satisfaction of an ambition that is contrary to the will of God. And of course failure is still very painful; but the pain is fruitful if it is part of God's

purpose. A failure, within God's purpose, is no longer really a failure.[2]

God's plan, both for the individual and the church as a whole, is the only important factor. We have been deceived into thinking that bigger is better, when in reality, only 2 percent of all Protestant churches have one thousand or more adults. "The United States is dominated by small churches, with the average church attracting less than 90 adults on a typical weekend."[3]

I believe the mindset of these small churches is that they do not have the people or resources to do anything but keep their sheep fed and content. They look at the megachurches with their thousands of people, twenty full-time staff members, sprawling campuses, and unlimited budgets, and conclude that *these are the movers and shakers of Christianity.*

But each church is called by our Lord to fulfill a specific purpose in His kingdom. "What is *our* destiny?" should be the cry of the people of God. Size is not the determining factor in fulfilling our purpose. One of the greatest military battles in Scripture was won by a small, seemingly insignificant group of people under Gideon's command—a man who was called by God as he was hiding in a winepress. Gideon's clan was the "weakest in Manasseh" and Gideon was the "least" in his family (Judges 6:15).

Our rational mind couples strength with great numbers, but God equates strength with weakness and a few committed people. The story of Israel demonstrates that God has always worked through a remnant so that He might receive the glory.

Our church is small—only about two hundred and fifty adults—but through us God has birthed thirty inner-city ministries staffed mainly by volunteers. We have no superheroes running the ministries; everyone has a vital part to play. No one is more important than the other; everyone just serves in his or her assigned role. This design is plainly seen in Scripture: "But in fact God has arranged the parts in the body, every one of them, just as he wanted them to be" (1 Corinthians 12:18).

Our church has been called to be a part of God's ground force. We thank God for the intercessors that have been called to pray and "soften up the ground" beforehand. But we serve another purpose; we are people on the ground—in the neighborhoods, projects, government, and workplaces—ready to execute hand-to-hand battles and take back ground from the enemy. The need for more ground forces has been a constant cry during the recent war in Iraq. *We could win if we only had enough soldiers on the ground.*

In the same way, we Christians could win in the battle for men's souls if we had enough soldiers willing to *leave the confines of their comfort zone and enter the arena of battle.* The U.S. Army has a motto that is very appropriate for the church: "Train as you fight." When we follow God into our destiny, the Holy Spirit will teach us and we will be trained as we fight the spiritual battle.

My hope in writing this book is to encourage the thousands of small churches like ours to step out in faith and follow Jesus into their destiny. God's kingdom will not be extended only by the few megachurches in our nation. Success also depends upon the small congregations of committed believers who are willing to engage their communities.

Each church's journey will be unique in how it is lived out, but there are some general principles that can be applied from our church's individual calling. So I hope you will check out the section at the end of each chapter called "Applying the Lessons." There I will sum up the universal truths that can be carried over from our experience to yours. If you let the Holy Spirit guide your destiny, I promise that you will find a new freedom that sets its own agenda for success.

A wonderful thing happens when we find our place of service in the body. Christianity becomes exciting, fulfilling, and full of good fruits. And we discover that in fulfilling His design for us—to be His hands extended to meet the needs of those around us—we have all we need to do just that. "Give, and it will be given to you. A good measure, pressed down, shaken together and running over, will be poured into your lap" (Luke 6:38).

The Call

Before I formed you in the womb I knew
you, before you were born I set you apart.
JEREMIAH 1:5

Why wasn't I happy? That thought kept me awake at night. My four children and a busy life kept me from that realization during the day. But at night, when my mind refused to shut down, I had to face the truth. I was going through the motions of being a happy suburban mom, but deep inside there was a gnawing feeling that I was missing something.

What could it be? I have everything I always wanted. My twenties had been difficult years with four children born in seven years, three major surgeries, and very tight finances with my husband in dental school. But now things were so different. We were living in a beautiful new home, my health was great, and my husband's dental practice was thriving.

That is how I felt one fall day in 1971 as I stood, dustcloth in hand, in the middle of the family room of our new home. Mellow music drifted from the radio, and I looked out through the patio doors to a crisp, beautiful day.

I have it all, I thought. *Everything is as it should be, and yet . . . where is the contentment and joy I should be feeling on a day like this?*

As if in commiseration, I heard Peggy Lee's voice on the radio singing the popular song "Is That All There Is?" The words hit home—that was *my* life Peggy Lee was singing about. Is that all there is to a marriage—kissing my husband good-bye in the morning and hello at night? Is that all there is to a family—this day-to-day routine of laundry, meals, and getting the kids ready for school? Is that all there is to a dream house in the suburbs—vacuuming, dusting, and scrubbing floors?

In my mind's eye I saw my life like a calendar, each page marking one year. A giant hand was flipping over leaf after leaf. I knew that when all the leaves were finally turned, there would be nothing at the end, nothing to give my life meaning. I spent my life worrying about the externals, the right house, clothes, and cars, hoping to cover up the hollow place within the center of my being. All my life I believed I would like myself if I *had* all the right things, and I almost succeeded in thinking I was happy and fulfilled—until now.

That point in 1971 marked the beginning of my conscious search for God. I bought a Bible, but had difficulty understanding much of it. My brother, who had just given his life to Christ, invited me to a prayer meeting at his house. As I looked around at the people singing praises to God, I was struck with this thought: *They all have something I don't have.* I now know that the Spirit of God revealed this to me, but at the time I thought it was my own insight.

When I went home that night, I knelt down by the side of my bed and asked Jesus to come into my life. He didn't—at least, not right away. In the past I had suffered periodic bouts of depression, but the next morning I awoke with the most overwhelming depression I had ever faced. My husband mentioned to me that I had gone to a prayer meeting and become worse than I was before.

I was confused. I knew that my prayer to Jesus had been sincere. I had asked Him to take over my life, and I totally submitted to whatever He had for me. I was tormented with the thought that God didn't want me—somehow I was "unacceptable." I decided that if God didn't want me, then I didn't want Him either. I tried to put my brief sojourn into Christianity out of my mind.

THE SURPRISE VISIT

On a Thursday night in January 1972, my husband, John, was working late. I was watching the ten o'clock news and exercising on the floor. Suddenly I "heard" a voice (perhaps in my thoughts) telling me in a gentle yet commanding tone to kneel down. I obeyed immediately. It seemed as if beams of light were entering my body. The light dispelled all the darkness that had followed me the past three weeks, and an overwhelming sense of love and gratitude flooded me. I began to praise and thank God in words that I couldn't believe were coming from me. (Later I learned they were from the Holy Spirit.) As quickly as it began the experience ended, but I was never the same.

I had no idea what had happened to me. Several days later, with some trepidation, I told John about my experience. He knew that I was usually a pretty logical person, especially concerning spiritual things. He concluded that I must have made contact with God in some way, but neither of us knew what to do about it.

I began attending weekly prayer meetings with a small group of new believers at my brother's house. I found that the Bible, which had previously been so confusing to me, suddenly made sense. In fact, every time I picked it up I felt the words were speaking just to me, and tears would often run down my cheeks.

A few weeks after this experience, as I was preparing breakfast for my children, my oldest son, John, asked me, "Mom, what happened to you?"

Before I could reply, Shannon, my second born, piped up, "Yes, you seem so different."

"What do you mean by different?" I asked.

"Well, you seem so happy—I don't know—just different," John ventured.

"Yes, and you're singing all the time," Shannon added.

"I am different because I gave my life to Jesus," I replied. "You know those prayer meetings I go to every week? Well, that's where we sing and praise Jesus."

To my surprise, both of them begged me to take them to the weekly meeting even though it was on a school night. I couldn't believe these were the same two kids who complained vehemently every Saturday morning about going to catechism classes. After consulting with my husband, I began taking them with me to our weekly meetings. Eventually, they too gave their lives to Christ and were baptized in the Holy Spirit.

During this time, my analytical husband was watching the three of us. It was only later that he told me any reservations he had about our weekly prayer meeting were overcome by my changed life. In his words, "You were so much easier to live with!" The reality of a real and living Savior had not only impacted my two oldest children, but my husband as well.

Don't Change Anything!

Three months later my husband also gave his life to Jesus, although he had a few stipulations. Unlike his wife, John was very happy with his life and he really didn't want it to change. He prayed something like this: "Dear Lord Jesus, please come into my life. I know I need you . . . but please don't change anything. Amen."

He had a successful dental practice, was on the board of directors of the Chicago Dental Society (the first step to becoming president), and was by nature a contented man. He also had a secret ambition to become a scratch golfer.

I'm so thankful that God doesn't take us at our word, because, of course, my husband's life did change—radically. He never became a scratch golfer. I'm sure the Lord laughs heartily when John has to play golf in one of our fund-raising events and shoots about 140.

> **I didn't realize that I was born again until a new Christian friend explained it to me six months later.**

John and I didn't understand what had happened to us. Neither of us had read the Bible much before this, and we were unfamiliar with biblical terminology. I didn't realize that I was born again until a new Christian friend explained it to me six months later. We were excited about Jesus. When our friends asked about the change in our lives, we freely told them about Him. We were unconcerned with denominations and doctrine, not knowing much about either of them.

God used our ignorance to lead us into what He had planned for us. We followed because we didn't know what else to do. We were as ignorant and confused as the disciples in John's gospel when Jesus asked them: "You do not want to leave too, do you?" Peter's reply echoed our thoughts and feelings: "Lord, to whom shall we go? You have the words of eternal life. We believe and know that you are the Holy One of God" (John 6:67–69).

We can take no credit for what has happened. All that has been done in our lives and the lives of others is a result of God's transforming grace. It has been and still is a tremendous journey of faith. There have been times of intense joy, but also times of great despair. Many discouraging days we wanted to quit—move to Colorado and enjoy the mountains. But the grace of God has kept us and is still keeping us in His will until we fulfill our purpose in Him.

Applying the Lessons

- *Don't expect God's transformation in people's lives to be like a formula. Each person's encounter with Him is unique and personal.*

- *Ensure that new converts bond to the person of Jesus—not the trappings of Christianity.*

- *Take no credit for what is done in your church. Carefully guard the glory and give it only to God, not to any man or program.*

Beginning

I came to Him;
not on my own,
forced by life's circumstances;
there was nowhere else to go.

All my life I drifted with the current,
sometimes in placid pools of pleasure,
more often
seized by hidden whirlpools,
or dashed on piercing rocks.

Finally, battered and bleeding,
I arrived at the ocean.
Nothing before me
but boundless blue-green space.
Then I saw it!

A Rock rising out of the sea;
a majestic steeple.
I threw myself upon it;
security, in the midst of churning sea.
I clung tightly to the Rock,
thankful, my hardships were past;
thankful, I reached my destination.

It was then I heard His voice
(whether from rock or wind I do not know)
This is not an end but a beginning!
"A beginning?
But where do I go from here?"
Now, said the voice ever so gently,
now we learn to swim upstream.

Small Beginnings

Do not despise this small beginning, for the eyes of the Lord rejoice to see the work begin.

ZECHARIAH 4:10 TLB

Even before we gave our life to Christ, He was leading John and me in ways we did not realize. We were attracted to some new model homes being built in our area. However, we could not agree. I liked a ranch-style model, and he preferred a larger tri-level. When he came home with a contract on the model he had chosen, I promptly ripped it to pieces. John patiently taped it back together and took it to the builder.

"Look what my wife thought of your contract," he mischievously said to the builder.

In spite of my protests, John's decision won out. One of the reasons he preferred that model was because of the spacious family room and the fifteen-foot bar off to the side. We loved to entertain, and this would be the ultimate party room.

As usual, God had other ideas for this home. The large family room became the meeting place for our congregation, and the bar was useful to display our gospel tracts. The smaller model I had preferred never could have held the eighty people who ultimately came weekly to our home.

Friends were impressed by the change in our lives and asked if they could join us for prayer and worship. We began to meet on Wednesday nights, but on Sunday mornings we all went back to the denominational churches we had always attended. We had no intention of becoming a church; we just wanted to fellowship and worship together.

For four years we met in our family room, and scores of people passed through our home during that time. We saw many exciting and miraculous answers to prayer. This was at the height of the charismatic movement, and people went to any meeting where the Holy Spirit was active. A Catholic priest, a Christian and Missionary Alliance pastor, and several Christian Reformed pastors were regulars at our Wednesday night meetings.

One of these pastors was a full-time staff member at the World Home Bible League located in our village of South Holland, Illinois. He was in charge of the Bibles for India project. Many years later he told us that he was attracted to our meetings because he could see that our meeting had been planted by the Holy Spirit. His analytical mind decided to see how the Holy Spirit formed a church, and then apply those same methods to his work in India.

He had little success in India before this time. But as he applied the principles he saw illustrated by our little house church, he was instrumental in raising up three hundred fifty self-supporting churches with native pastors in one year! God was using our little group in ways we didn't know or even understand at the time.

SHIFTING GEARS

We were enjoying God and gave no long-term thought to where He was taking us. However, one significant change occurred during this time. Our core group of about forty people left their individual denominations and together began attending the Christian and Missionary Alliance church in our town. The minister and his wife were a godly couple who had just returned from years of ministry in Vietnam.

Our prayer group met on Wednesday and a few other nights during the week to listen to teaching tapes and to fellowship, but on Sunday we all went to the Alliance church. We probably would have done this forever if the pastor hadn't taken us aside one morning after the service.

I was still basking in the afterglow of the worship service and prophetic teaching, when our pastor approached us. His first words broke into my reverie and brought me back to reality with a thud.

"I have been praying about your fellowship and have the strong impression that God wants you to incorporate and become a church," he began.

We were totally unprepared for this. My husband patiently explained to him that *we didn't want to become a church*. We were a prayer group and definitely wanted to stay that way. We were having fun as we were, and none of us had any desire to take this next step.

"But you *are* a church, and you have to accept God's will," was his reply to John. "God has given you these people, and you are responsible for them. You need to accept your responsibility."

We were both stunned by his words, and it took some time for my husband to accept that he was a "pastor" and responsible for the lives of about sixty people. So much for his life not changing! I'm thankful we couldn't hear the laughter in heaven. After a brief time of wrestling with God, John submitted and accepted his responsibility.

Breaking the Rules

One reason my husband resisted this counsel at first is a strong conviction that he holds to this day. As he often says, "One thing the world does not need is another church! But it does need a *true expression of the heart of Jesus Christ.*"

We live in a town that has many churches; our town's water tower even has "Praying Hands" painted on it. In our village we still abide by the blue laws, originally enacted by the Puritans in seventeenth-century Connecticut to regulate moral behavior (especially what people must or must not do on the Sabbath). There is no liquor sold in our village, and all stores are closed on Sundays. Restaurants are the only businesses open on the Sabbath.

We love this about our village. Sundays are quiet days, when families can really enjoy being together. When we first moved to

South Holland, forty-two years ago, many churches were still in legalistic bondage to these rules. Households had very elaborate rules for what could and couldn't be done on Sundays. Friends have told me they were not allowed to do anything that caused them to perspire, like jumping rope or roller-skating. They could sit and read a book. Usually they slept through the afternoons till church started on Sunday evening. All Sunday meals had to be prepared the day before.

So imagine, if you can, God planting a church like ours in the middle of this extremely conservative village. For many years we were accused of being a cult. One of the major points of contention was the fact that our main meeting was and still is on Wednesday night. We did not "keep holy the Sabbath" in their estimation.

We didn't start out in any deliberate way to break tradition. It just so happened that when we moved out of our home into our first rented building, we could only use it on Wednesdays. It was several years before we understood that the Lord intended that we keep this as our main meeting day. The Scripture verse God gave us is from Romans 14:5, where Paul is discussing the difference between weak and strong faith: "One man considers one day more sacred than another; another man considers *every day alike*. Each one should be fully convinced in his own mind."

We were fully convinced in our own minds; we did not believe that Christianity was a *place* we went to on Sunday morning, but a *life* that we lived every day. What did it matter what day we worshiped—as long as we were not neglecting to meet together? (Hebrews 10:25).

It is amazing what hostility this policy has generated in some Christians. Many people have told us they would come to our church if we would only have a Sunday morning church service. We had to decide whether to follow God's blueprint for our church or man's ideas of religion. God wanted us to live out our Christianity every day of the week, to deal a death blow to the religious rituals that convince a man he is right with God even though his daily walk is self-motivated.

> **We had to decide whether to follow God's blueprint for our church or man's ideas of religion.**

Jesus faced that same hostility with the Pharisees. In Matthew 12, He has a showdown with them over the Sabbath. They were upset that His disciples had picked grain on the Sabbath.

> At that time Jesus went through the grainfields on the Sabbath. His disciples were hungry and began to pick some heads of grain and eat them. When the Pharisees saw this, they said to him, "Look! Your disciples are doing what is unlawful on the Sabbath" (Matthew 12:1–2).

Jesus defended His disciples with the example of King David, but He knew that His words were falling on deaf ears:

> If you had known what these words mean, "I *desire mercy, not sacrifice*," you would not have condemned the innocent. For the Son of Man is Lord of the Sabbath. (Matthew 12:7–8)

To paraphrase Jesus' words: "I am really not interested in your religious exercises, which make you feel better but do nothing to advance my kingdom. My desire is that you would see the poor and needy all around you and be moved by my compassion. Pour your lives out for these—the least—and you will truly be doing my will."

Jesus left that place and went into the synagogue. The Pharisees saw a chance to catch Him in the act of healing on the Sabbath, which was also against their law.

> Going on from that place, he went into their synagogue, and a man with a shriveled hand was there. Looking for a reason to accuse Jesus, they asked him, "Is it lawful to heal on the Sabbath?" (Matthew 12:9–10).

Jesus once again tried to explain to the Pharisees that acts of mercy were not a violation of the Sabbath, but were actually what God preferred. They saw the keeping of the law as an end in itself rather than a way of honoring God. Jesus knew He was sealing his fate when He completely restored the man's withered hand. "The Pharisees went out and plotted how they might kill Jesus" (Matthew 12:14).

LEGALISM VS. SERVICE

Why did the Pharisees react so strongly against Jesus' acts of mercy? Why do Christians today react so strongly against a church not meeting on Sunday? A recent interview with David Van-Cronkhite in *Charisma* magazine offers some interesting clues.

David left a lucrative career as a CEO of a computer systems company to work full time with the poor of Atlanta. At one point the Sunday service was halted so the many homeless people in the area could live inside the church building. Rather than rejoicing that they were able to give shelter to so many of the poor, the church people reacted because their service was temporarily halted. As a result, the monthly tithe income dropped from $40,000 to $3,000. David says that the Sunday morning service is the "cash cow" of the church.

Eventually David resumed the Sunday morning service, but he says the church isn't centered on it. "It's not about Sunday morning—it's about what we are doing during the week."[1]

Throughout history people have tended to be religious in nature. It is so much easier to follow rules than the Holy Spirit of God. In the wilderness a cloud led the Israelites during the day and a fire led them by night. Today we have the blessed Holy Spirit who has taken up residence within us. This is a fulfillment of Jesus' promise to the disciples as He prepared to return to heaven. "It is for your good that I am going away. Unless I go away, the Counselor will not come to you; but if I go, I will send him to you. . . . When he, the Spirit of truth, comes, he [not rules] will guide you into all truth" (John 16:7, 13).

Very early on in our ministry, I met the wrath of the church legalists. A young couple in our church had twins, and the mom and babies were scheduled to come home from the hospital on a Monday morning. This couple had recently suffered a devastating financial loss and were without insurance. Our church paid all their hospital bills, and now we wanted to prepare the house for their homecoming.

So on the Sunday morning before their scheduled return home, several ladies and I took cleaning supplies and a vacuum over to their house. We enjoyed a day of fellowship together as we dusted, mopped, and prepared the nursery for the new babies. We left with such a sense of fulfillment that we were totally unprepared for the phone calls that came the next morning.

Some people were upset that we had used Sunday to clean the couple's house; they felt we had not "kept holy" the Sabbath. I was still a young Christian at the time, and I couldn't believe a person would actually find fault with such an obvious act of mercy for a fellow human being. In retrospect, I suppose it isn't that surprising.

Like many today, the Pharisees believed that they were God's defense team. What Jesus said to them in Matthew 12:7, "If you had known what these words mean, 'I desire mercy, not sacrifice,' you would not have condemned the innocent," could just as well be spoken to some elements in the church today. Truly God is not concerned with *when* and *where* we worship. He is concerned about how we live our life each day and whether we are reaching out to the brother or sister who is in need of love, food, clothing, or housing.

Many people feel that when they attend church on Sunday morning they are somehow fulfilling a deep need in God's heart. They have done their duty—given their sacrifice—till the next Sunday. They don't stop to think that rule-keeping is more akin to the Pharisees than Jesus.

As Jesus walked near the pool of Bethesda, the Holy Spirit led Him to one man who had been an invalid for thirty-eight years. His heart of compassion was drawn toward this man and He healed him of his infirmity. Jesus told him to pick up his mat and walk. To carry his mat on the Sabbath was forbidden, and not surprisingly it drew the chastisement of the Pharisees. Rather than glorify God for the miraculous healing, they were more determined than ever to put an end to this Jesus who openly flaunted their religious rules. "So, because Jesus was doing these things on the Sabbath, the Jews persecuted him. . . . For this reason the Jews tried all the harder to kill him" (John 5:16, 18).

Legalism sought to kill Jesus then and just as surely kills Him today. Jesus came to reveal the Father to the people because their idea of God was what they saw mirrored by the Pharisees, whose traditions focused on purity laws concerning washing, eating, tithing, and Sabbath observance. "In their zeal for the Law they almost deified it and their attitude became merely external, formal and mechanical. They laid stress, not upon the righteousness of an action, but upon its formal correctness."[2]

We all have a tendency to seek out safety and security in life, especially in our religion. So we create tradition and habits that become familiar to us. When we become too ingrained in tradition, however, we are no longer trusting God to keep us safe and secure. He desires that we move out of our comfort zone into a radical Christianity, because when we are in a place that calls for risk and deep faith, there we will find our safety and security in Him alone.

In our case, God did not want us to become just another traditional church centered on a Sunday morning service. As Jesus revealed the true nature of the Father to the Jews, in the same way He wanted us to become a true expression of the heart of God: a heart that cries for mercy, not sacrifice, a heart that sees the one with the withered hand and reaches out in love to touch and heal.

Of course, we didn't know this then. We were simply following a cloud that was moving. We sure didn't want to lose sight of it—then we wouldn't know which way to go on this adventure with God.

Applying the Lessons

- *Be more concerned about God's leading than what is currently "acceptable" to others. Play to an audience of one.*

- *Be open to new developments orchestrated by God, even if they bring more hassles and responsibilities.*

- *Embrace biblical principles, but shun legalism like the plague.*

We Did It for You, Lord?

We did it for you, Lord.
We thought you would like a golden tower,
inscribed with your Name.
Bells announcing time to worship and
organ pipes vibrating celestial harmonies.
We did it for you.

    For centuries men and women
have dedicated themselves to serving you,
in austere gray or black clothing.
Solemn!
Unsmiling!
It is serious business, and
they did it for you.

    Men have marched to war
to defend your truth.
Burned up towns and
witches at the stake;
held inquisitions, tortured infidels.
They did it for you.

    We have established special schools
for the study of your Word;
institutions that drain away faith,
leaving words without Spirit.
We did it for you.

    On Sunday morning,
when we would rather stay in bed,
we drag ourselves to church,
to worship and pray and
nod and squirm on the hard wood,
wondering when the sermon will end.
We do it for you.

We give our money
to build more churches, so
more people will come
to worship and pray and
nod and squirm on the hard wood,
wondering when the sermon will end.
We do it for you, Lord.
Don't we?
Lord?

3 Following the Cloud

By day the Lord went ahead of them in a pillar of cloud to guide them on their way.
Exodus 13:21

The Christian and Missionary Alliance pastor who counseled us to incorporate as a church had his eyes fixed on the *kingdom of God*. He knew that if we heeded his counsel, about forty or fifty people would leave his small church. Most pastors in his position would have concluded that it was in our best interest to stay in an established church. After all, we were totally unqualified, by human standards, to pastor a church. But he was used of God to bring us to the next step of our journey.

In spite of our reservations, we began the process of incorporating and becoming a church. My husband was recognized as the pastor, but he decided early on against titles.

"A person changes when he has a title," he was fond of saying. "People will recognize those men that God has anointed." To this day, most people call him John, or Doc, since he is a practicing dentist.

Sadly, there are some in Christendom who are almost obsessed with titles. I've noticed in the advertisements for some Christian conferences that every speaker has at least one, two, possibly three titles. I often wonder when I see these: *Did God give you that title, or did man?* And it grieves me to think that some in the church have fallen prey to the world's philosophy—that titles give us greater validity and influence. Our true identity, the one that really counts, can only be found in the risen Christ, not in a title bestowed by men.

Paul did refer to himself as an apostle, but he made it clear that he was "sent not from men nor by man, but by Jesus Christ and God the Father" (Galatians 1:1). Paul also loved to refer to himself as "a servant of Christ Jesus" (Romans 1:1) and even as "a prisoner of Christ Jesus" (Philemon 1:1). Paul had a very clear understanding that he was first and foremost a *servant* of Christ, whose particular calling was as an apostle.

If we see that we are primarily called to be servants of Christ to the lost and hurting in this world, we will not be concerned about our title. Every believer should long for the day when the Master will say to him, "Well done, good and faithful *servant!*" (Matthew 25:21). I don't think titles are going to have anything to do with our heavenly reward; our reward will reflect our faithfulness to our calling.

A well-read Christian magazine featured an article about a woman who is filling stadiums around the United States. Usually introduced with the imposing title of "prophetess," this woman was recently married in a very lavish ceremony befitting royalty and was given a seven-carat diamond ring. Although many pages were devoted to her story, only about a third of a page in that same magazine was written to record the death of one of the greatest men of this last century: Bill Bright, founder of Campus Crusade for Christ International.

Bill was a true servant of God, who lived a modest lifestyle so more money could be filtered into the kingdom of God. The write-up about him didn't mention any diamond jewelry, but it did mention the 5.1 billion people that have been exposed to the gospel through his *Jesus* Film Project and his *Four Spiritual Laws* tract that has been translated into two hundred languages.[1] All his life people referred to him only as Bill. He was one of God's faithful servants.

IDENTIFYING GODLY LEADERS

In our new church fellowship we functioned for five years without titles, but God did raise up faithful men anointed with His Spirit who were eventually installed as elders. Our pastor friend, the one who established many churches in India, said he never chose a pastor or elders at the beginning of a church formation. He would watch the fledgling church for several years and notice who began to function in leadership without being recognized with a title. Soon it became evident whom the Lord had gifted and chosen to lead the new congregation.

We found through trial and error over the years that the most charismatic person did not always make the best leader. Often these charismatic types draw people to themselves rather than to Jesus. We also made some errors in judgment with people who appeared to be very dedicated to the church. Only after they left—usually taking some of our members with them—did we realize that we had chosen them on the basis of gifting rather than character. It took many years to understand the importance of choosing *servant leaders* with a heart for God's people.

God Would Make a Way

Our first challenge as a church came after an especially well-attended Wednesday evening. The village attorney called my husband to convey several complaints from neighbors in our cul-de-sac. Some were about the sheer number of cars around our house and a few concerned parking violations.

"Now, I know that with your first amendment rights, we can't force you to move the prayer meeting out of your home, but if there was a fire in your cul-de-sac, the trucks couldn't get in," he told my husband.

"I would love to get the meeting out of our home," John replied. "We have about eighty people attending, and we are bulging at the seams. I tried to secure the old village-owned American Legion Hall, but they refused to give me the building on a weekly basis."

"I'll get right back to you," the lawyer replied.

Ten minutes later he called back. "You can have the Legion Hall every Wednesday night indefinitely, per the mayor's instructions."

John was speechless!

It was a powerful lesson for our little group. We had tried for months to find another place to meet, without success. God used our neighbors' complaints to accomplish His purpose and show us that He would go before us and make a way. Our trust level in God jumped up one hundred points, and we were on our way.

The cloud was moving and we had to follow or be left behind. From 1976 to 1988 we met in three different buildings. God divinely directed each move. The last two buildings we rented were schools that had been closed for lack of students. This was a blessing because it meant that we didn't have to move our sound system and instruments each week. We had all the benefits of ownership but none of the hassles.

John never wanted to own a building. He felt the care and maintenance of a building would take too much time and money away from the calling of God on our church. As usual, I saw things differently from John. I thought it would be wonderful to have our own building and also to have services on Sunday morning. We had an intense discussion (some call it an argument) on this subject as we drove home from dinner with friends one night. As I walked into the entry hall of our home, I was mentally reloading my guns for a second round on the subject. But God chose that moment to break into my thoughts with the words: *And they wanted a king so they would be like all the other nations.*

God knew precisely how to get my attention. I had been studying First and Second Samuel for months. I knew that the Israelites had angered God with their desire for a human king so they would be like all the other nations (1 Samuel 8:5–8). God revealed my heart in that moment and showed me that I wanted a Sunday morning service and our own building so *we would be like the other churches in our town.* I suppose I was tired of being different. And I didn't like being accused of being a cult because we were different.

OBEDIENCE TO HIS PLAN

It isn't that there is anything wrong with a Sunday morning service—it's a wonderful time to get together and fellowship. But God was leading us in a different direction, and He wanted our obedience to His plan. I had to repent of my desire to be like other churches and submit to God's will for our lives. After this revelation, John and I prayed together for His direction and purpose, both in our individual lives and in the life of the church.

With this historical background, you can understand why John was so surprised when a Christian businessman named Lawrence VanSomeren approached him in 1987 with an offer to give us ten acres of land and a Christian school. My husband's immediate response was an emphatic NO!

This man had already established a Christian school, and the church that had been meeting in the school's gym had moved out. His offer to us came out of a desire for our church to give covering and oversight to the school. He made it clear that he wanted us to have a very hands-on approach to the school, giving both direction and leadership to it.

He was not deterred by John's answer. He simply replied, "God said to give the property and school to your church."

"Well, God didn't tell me to accept it," John shot back.

Lawrence was persistent and continued to call John and relate what the Lord told him. John was equally persistent in his refusal to accept his offer.

"At least spend some time praying about it," Lawrence implored John.

Finally John gathered our church elders and their wives together to discuss the offer. We were all unanimous in our opinion—we were *not* to have a permanent building, even though the building and property being offered were free of debt. But we did decide to take a year to pray and fast about the offer and then make our final decision.

So many people assume an offer like this is too good to refuse and so must be of God. Why waste time praying about it? But we didn't want to lose the unique vision God had for us and be sidetracked by the responsibility of maintaining a building and a school. We did not want to be encumbered with additional worries or end up using our finances to keep the school afloat.

Another factor that fueled our reluctance was John's view of Christian schools. His reasoning was that he would rather influence the secular school system than get involved with a Christian school. He had served on our public school board for many years and felt Christians should become more active in local concerns. It is true that too many Christians want to withdraw into a little cocoon where they feel safe from the world. In so doing, they forfeit all opportunity to impact the world for Jesus. John was quite well known in our community for his work on many village boards and his strong Christian principles.

At the end of our year of prayer, the elders and their wives met to discuss the issue. Surprisingly, God had changed each one of us. Again we unanimously agreed—to accept the offer. The cloud had stopped over this property, and we finally got the message.

At that time the school consisted of kindergarten through grade twelve. It was quite small—about one hundred twenty-five students. From John's school board experience, he knew that it was impossible to give a good education to such a broad base of students with limited funds. For that reason he decided to disband the high school and that caused some shock tremors within the Christian community.

Like many Christian schools, ours was not accredited. John hired Karen Pender, a young woman with a master's degree in education, and she promptly set out to prepare the school for accreditation. "If we are going to have a Christian school, then it has to be the best in order to reflect Christ" was my husband's philosophy.

After many years of hard work, our school earned seven years' accreditation, the highest possible. Eventually, our benefactor decided we also needed a church building, since we had been meeting in the school's gymnasium and had outgrown it. He mentioned to John that they should get together with the elders to discuss building a church facility.

"How much do you think it will cost?" John asked.

"Oh, about eight hundred thousand dollars," Lawrence replied.

My husband quickly said, "Anytime we talk over two hundred thousand dollars, I get nervous."

"Fine," said Lawrence, "then don't come to the meeting!"

Again, our main concern was that we would be so tied up financially that we could not support our growing ministries to the poor. By this time we had already established Harvey House, a discipleship center for men from addictive backgrounds. We didn't want to fall into the trap of many churches, being "building poor" and unable to invest in other ministry opportunities.

George Barna relates that poverty is a growing problem in America. Approximately thirty million Americans, 40 percent of them children, live below the poverty level. He reminds us that "the Church was called by Christ to care for the least of all people, and to be known by the quality of its love. . . . Despite these glaringly apparent needs, churches across the country are minimally involved in addressing this issue. For every dollar spent on ministry to the poor, the typical church spends more than five dollars on buildings and maintenance."[2]

Often as soon as a church starts experiencing some success, the leadership's first thought is to build a new eye-catching building to attract more members. The intent is usually to target the affluent suburbanites, convincing them through various seeker strategies that their church isn't that different from the world. The mindset is to *get people into the building* to be ministered to rather than challenging church members to go out into the harvest fields. The high mortgage often means that members must give large amounts of money to the church building, thereby siphoning finances away from any outreaches to the poor and disadvantaged.

Feathering Our Own Nests

The prophet Haggai was sent by God to prophesy to the Jews who had returned to Jerusalem from their exile in Babylon. They began with great zeal to rebuild the temple, but the hostility of neighboring tribes and other factors caused them to turn to private affairs and to worship among the ruins. God, through Haggai, rebuked them for their lack of concern for His temple and said this was the reason for their many problems.

> Is it a time for you yourselves to be living in your paneled houses, while this house remains a ruin? (Haggai 1:4)
> "What you brought home, I blew away. Why?" declares the Lord Almighty. "Because of my house, which remains a ruin, while each of you is busy with his own house" (Haggai 1:9).

In Haggai's day, God dwelt in a physical temple, but today God does not dwell in houses made by men (Acts 7:48). Instead, we are the temples of the Holy Spirit. We think that God delights in the beautiful buildings we build for Him, but the truth is that God really doesn't care about buildings. He cares about people. One day all those buildings will tumble down and be destroyed, but the people we have brought to Him will continue to bring glory to Him into eternity.

To paraphrase Haggai's words, why are we so busy pouring money into programs and buildings while the true kingdom of God—the people—are neglected? Why is each pastor concerned only with his own church? Why do we deceive ourselves that we are doing this for God, when we are really feeding our egos? Why do we place so much emphasis on large and/or beautiful buildings and such little emphasis on working with the poor and needy around us?

If we hold true to the vision God has given us, then He is free to give us what we need to fulfill that vision.

Our church building did get built, but without debt. I believe that if we hold true to the vision God has given us, then He is free to give us what we need to fulfill that vision.

John created a committee called the "Men of Issachar" to oversee our church finances. In the Bible these men of Issachar were men "who understood the times and knew what Israel should do" (1 Chronicles 12:32). John asked some successful Christian businessmen to be on the committee. These are committed men who "understand the times" and have given us invaluable counsel and help. Most of them attend other churches, but want to support us in our work with the poor. Because of their help, my husband is free to fulfill his calling and not be tied down with financial cares.

Over the years these men have supervised the construction of a large day-care facility and two substantial additions to the Christian school. The day care not only provides a secure environment for children but it also funded the additions to the school. We've also purchased a large building on the edge of our property to serve as a meeting place for our multicultural youth church.

The campus has grown over the years, but none of the buildings has tied us up financially. The grace of God, working through gifted, godly people, made it possible. As a result, we can continue to bring His redemptive love to the outcasts of society. The cloud continues to move, and our ministries to the poor continue to grow and flourish. All praise to Him!

Applying the Lessons

- *Fast and pray as a group for a designated time before making big changes in direction.*

- *Build buildings to serve your church's ministry needs, not to impress visitors.*

- *Seek creative ways to fund your building/ministry needs. Look to God to supply your needs and be willing to partner with other godly leaders that He sends your way.*

Why This Waste?

The fragrance filled the house,
rising from His perfumed feet,
permeating the room and
even filling the stingy nostrils
of Judas, the accountant;
a practical man, who knew
the value of a dollar,
but not the eternal value
of giving all, when it was foolish,
impractical, and
would not yield a good return.

Those who look for an even exchange
cannot enter the kingdom,
where the exchange is very,
very, uneven.
One perfect sinless life,
exchanged for one imperfect,
sinful creature.
Very, very uneven!
God wasted His best.

"Why this waste?"
Judas questioned, anticipating
the angels' cries as
blood poured from the side
of the perfect sacrifice.
"Why this waste?"
they screamed silently to heaven,
where only the Father knew . . .
and waited.

4 The Shepherd As Leader

Be shepherds of God's flock that is under your care, serving as overseers—not because you must, but because you are willing, as God wants you to be; not greedy for money, but eager to serve; not lording it over those entrusted to you, but being examples to the flock.

1 PETER 5:2–3

Early on we decided that no one in our church would receive a salary; we would all function as volunteers. John took his cue from the apostle Paul, who was a tentmaker by trade. In a letter to the Corinthian church, Paul acknowledged, "Those who preach the gospel *should* receive their living from the gospel" (1 Corinthians 9:14). However, Paul did not choose to use his right so he could offer the gospel "free of charge" (1 Corinthians 9:18).

In a letter to the Thessalonians, Paul said: "We worked night and day, laboring and toiling so that we would not be a burden to any of you. We did this, not because we do not have the right to such help, but in order to make ourselves *a model for you to follow*" (2 Thessalonians 3:8–9).

John was such a "model" for the leaders in our church to follow. He worked a forty-hour week at dentistry and still fulfilled his role in the church so that other working men and women could not say they were "too busy" to be actively involved. We knew that everyone in the church is equally responsible to use the gifts and talents God has given for the edification of the body. John's constant refrain has been, "If we are going to be successful, we all must pull our share of the load."

LEADING BY EXAMPLE

Too often the unspoken attitude of the congregation has been: "We are paying our pastor to preach our sermons, pray our prayers, and live an exemplary life before God. After all, he has the time, while we have to make a living. Our job is to evaluate how well he is doing." In this way, the Sunday morning service becomes another spectator event with one man performing and the rest of the church giving him a score for his performance.

When people find out that John does not receive a salary, it changes their perspective. First of all, it gives us immediate validity, especially among the African-American population with whom we work. Many African-American men see the pastor as a man driving a Lincoln at the expense of the women in the church who struggle to pay their tithe.

At the drug abuse center where I have taught a Bible study since 1982, the fact that we don't receive a salary is a great boost to the trust factor of the residents. They know, by word of mouth, that we only come there because God has sent us to tell them they are loved—not for any monetary compensation.

It is also a way to model the servanthood of Christ to them. "Just as the Son of Man did not come to be served, but to serve" (Matthew 20:28), we want to model true Christianity to them right from the beginning. As a result, we see them coming into the church with a desire to serve others still trapped in their sin and addiction.

We are imprinted by example at our new birth in much the same way a baby duckling is imprinted by the figure present at its birth. Those who have come from the lower echelons of society are often attracted to the prosperity gospel, but through the example of volunteer leaders they learn that actually the highest honor in God's kingdom is to be a servant.

THE SHEPHERD AS LEADER • 45

Preaching Without Constraint

Another benefit of not receiving a salary is the freedom it gives us to preach the truth without constraint. We do not have to worry about offending those who only want their ears tickled (2 Timothy 4:3). We can "speak the truth in love" as God leads us (Ephesians 4:15).

There have been times when something we said caused such an offense that a few people left. While we always grieve their leaving, we don't back down from what God has instructed us to share. In our situation, having people leave does not cause our salary to decrease in any way, because zero from zero is still zero!

Some churches are run by their boards, and the pastor has to keep everybody happy if he wants to retain his position and his security. We know pastors who are just hanging on till retirement, speaking the platitudes that keep everybody in the congregation comfortable because they don't want to rock the security boat.

A pastor recently surprised my husband by saying, "I sure envy you."

"You envy me?" John replied. "Why?"

"Because you can preach the truth with your people and they can't threaten you."

"Would you preach differently if your salary weren't at stake?" John asked him.

"You better believe it! That's why I envy you," he sadly replied.

So much of the church system is set up to encourage "hirelings," the hired hands of any trade. Jesus talked about them in John 10:12–13, and said that they couldn't care for the sheep like a true shepherd because they looked after them only with the motive to be paid. When things got tough or dangerous, the hirelings would be gone. Sadly, some leaders of churches fall into that category. They serve mostly out of self-interest, not a genuine concern for the congregation.

Novice pastors may be called to a small or struggling church, but most of them do not want to stay there. Their eye is more than likely on that large, well-paying church in their denominational structure. If they get there, they figure, they will have truly achieved success in their profession. Having been given false goals that mimic worldly success, they don't realize that in God's kingdom our success is not in the size of our churches but in the health of our sheep.

In God's kingdom our success is not in the size of our churches but in the health of our sheep.

Charles Colson in his cutting-edge book *Being the Body*, mentions, "Most pastors are under pressure to grow their churches; that's how we measure success. Businesses penetrate new markets by giving people what they want. The temptation is great for the church to do the same: to offer pleasure, but in a spiritualized form. . . . Give people what it takes to get them into the tent; then let them have the whole message."[1] This may be good business strategy, but bad theology and a deceptive practice.

Building Trust Takes Time

John is the oldest pastor in our village of about forty churches. He has seen many pastors come and go. Often they were not concerned about shepherding the people in their congregation but moving up in the denomination. When the more lucrative offer came, they were gone without a backward glance. This is not to say these men were not good, caring men—many are—but this is the model that was set before them.

In many cases it is denominational protocol for the pastor to stay three, five, maybe seven years, and then move on. We have known wonderful, humble pastors who had a deep care and concern for their sheep but they were not allowed to stay. Eventually they were forced to accept a position at another church.

George Barna found "that senior pastors typically experience their major impact during the fifth through fourteenth years of tenure. However, the average tenure of a senior pastor in American churches has dropped to just *four years*."[2] As a result, most pastors are never around to see the fruit of their labor. They are always starting over again.

This trend is also very difficult on their families. Sometimes it takes a few years for a pastor's wife to feel at home in a new place.

Just about the time she has made some solid friendships, she must pack up and move, starting the whole process over again. The same can be said of the children in the family.

My family moved frequently because of my father's job, so I know the drawbacks personally. I hated standing before my new school class and being introduced. I stood there—shoulders rounded, hands clasped tightly, and eyes cast down—while curious eyes studied me. For years, even as an adult, I wondered why I hated introductions. I also tended to be a loner because I didn't want to put all that energy into establishing a friendship only to have to leave again.

When pastors move frequently, they never develop relationships within the community and therefore do not impact the neighborhood. I know from our experience that it takes years to establish a reputation as a man of God.

My husband was recently honored with the first "Man of Faith" award in our village and also the first educational enrichment award from a secular high school district for his contribution to education. The recognition my husband receives now and the trust of other pastors has come through thirty-four years of involvement in the community. Just "being there" is sometimes the most important function of a pastor. Not too long ago, a couple we hadn't seen in six years came back to our service. The wife's first words were, "I'm so glad you are still here."

TEACHING IS NOT SHEPHERDING

When Jesus went through the towns and villages teaching, preaching, and healing, the crowds moved him to compassion "because they were harassed and helpless, *like sheep without a shepherd*" (Matthew 9:36). In those times, as today, there was no shortage of teachers. In fact, it was the teachers—the scribes, Pharisees, and Sadducees—who most opposed Jesus. But there was a shortage of true shepherds who would lay down their ambition, their paycheck, their time, and their lives so that the sheep would be fed.

When we think of "feeding the sheep," the word *teaching*

immediately pops into our mind. But we have observed in our ministry that many people are unable to transfer the teaching they heard from the pulpit on Sunday morning into their daily life. They need *shepherds* (mentors—in today's language) to help them live out the gospel daily in the trenches of the world.

Over the years we have come to understand that each person filters what he or she hears from the pulpit through several screens: their varied experiences, their need at the moment, wounds in their spirit, and their motivational gift. Because of these variables, none of us hears the same message that someone else hears.

Our churches in North America are structured after the American educational system; a teacher stands and lectures, and the students supposedly absorb the information and then apply it to a test or a life situation. As a former high school teacher, I know that most of the children in the classroom don't "get it" without some one-on-one help. Our church began a homework mentoring ministry among the disadvantaged population we serve because we know that these kids won't learn in the typical classroom. And it is working. A school that we have mentored in our target suburb is the only school in that town that is now off the scholastic watch list.

If you look at the statistics on the American church today, you have to conclude that we don't "get it" either. We certainly have not "salted" our communities and kept out corruption. Christian divorce is at the same rate as the world's, the number of Christian men hooked on pornography is alarming, and pastors are leaving their calling at surprising rates. Most Christians don't possess a biblical worldview, which is like a filter through which they see life. Since they lack this filter, they are unable to make decisions based on biblical principles. Instead, they act out of emotion, pressure, or past experience.

When your husband leaves you for another woman, and you are about to go down for the third time, you don't want a "teaching" from your pastor; you want a shepherd who will *be there* for you and your family.

Just recently a family returned to our church. They originally left to go to a larger church with a great Bible teacher and a Sunday morning service. What brought them back to us was a devastating problem with one of their children. While they appreciated the great teaching they were getting, they needed even more the ministry of a caring body of believers and the stability of a shepherd leader standing with them in their difficult situation.

George Barna found that the majority of those who go into full-time ministry do so because they feel they have a gift for teaching. He also discovered that teaching and leading are related but distinct giftings. The troubling finding is that "most senior pastors serving churches today are not truly leaders, although they hold a position of leadership. Only 5 percent of senior pastors say they have the gift of leadership."[3]

Good teaching is certainly important, even essential, for those of us who want to follow the Lord Jesus in obedience. When we were a fledgling church, our only access to good teaching was through tapes and books. Frequently we gathered up to three times a week to listen to a tape series by anointed teachers. Without this teaching we most certainly would have gone astray. I thank God for these wonderful men and women. We soon realized, however, that many people needed one-on-one ministry to help them *walk out in a practical way* what they had heard in the teaching.

The Importance of Relationship

My concern is that many churches honestly believe good teaching and great programs are all that is needed for the congregation to flourish spiritually. We have elevated education to the same status as it enjoys in the world. The commercial frequently seen on TV, "The More You Know," features celebrities talking about learning as if it is the solution to all our problems. It isn't! We need relationships with caring, wise people who will take us by the hand and walk with us—the way Jesus walked with His disciples. He taught them many things, but mostly they learned by watching Him in various life situations.

One evening I was sitting in our church watching the graduation of Daniel, one of our Harvey House men. He was graduating

from an eighteen-month program for men with addictive backgrounds. On the stage with him were his pastor, the director of
the program, his mentor, his counselor, and his house church
leader. I turned to the visiting speaker next to me and said, "Look
at what it takes to bring a man out of his addiction and into the
fullness of the kingdom." It takes more than just good teaching,
which they receive; it takes men walking with him until he is able
to stand on his own.

Because of our infatuation with knowledge as the key to success, we often elevate good teachers to almost a godlike status. We
are convinced that his words hold the answers to all of life's problems, so we eagerly devour his books and his latest teaching. His
sheep lead people to their teacher rather than to Jesus. They build
up the kingdom of their teacher rather than the kingdom of God.
They use money to spread the word of their teacher through radio
programs, books, and television shows. Meanwhile, the poor and
needy are still harassed and struggle along without a compassion-
ate shepherd to encourage them.

I do enjoy a few shows on Christian television, but many times
I have to turn off the set because I find it disturbing. It bothers me
to watch a man or woman of God strutting up and down the stage,
hand raised in the air, loudly declaring "lordship" over everything
from sickness to death. And from all appearances, the people in
the audience love it. Many today have bought the message of the
TV commercial: Knowledge is power. It is so seductive, because
by and large we want power, not humility. We want personal victory, not submission. Seeing our desires granted is what matters,
not denying ourselves for the sake of the kingdom.

JESUS' REQUIREMENTS FOR LEADERSHIP

Jesus didn't strut! He walked in humble submission to the will
of His Father. When He did raise his voice in righteous anger, it
was to declare: "It is written . . . 'My house will be called a house
of prayer,' but you are making it a 'den of robbers'" (Matthew
21:13).

Jesus clearly laid down the requirements of leadership to His ambitious, quarrelsome disciples:

> You know that the rulers of the Gentiles lord it over them, and their high officials exercise authority over them. Not so with you. Instead, whoever wants to become great among you must be your servant, and whoever wants to be first must be your slave—just as the Son of Man did not come to be served, but to serve, and to give his life as a ransom for many. (Matthew 20:25–28)

The pastor of a congregation is not there to be put on a pedestal and served . . . the pastor is the servant! In the typical church structure, pastors spend much of their time isolated in their offices, preparing to deliver the "word" during the weekly service. They appear on Sunday morning, bestow their knowledge on the gathering, and then leave to go back into isolation or on to their latest round of conferences. They have functioned in their gift, but unfortunately their job isn't finished.

The people under their care still need help in walking out what they have been taught. If the church is so large that the pastor cannot do all the mentoring himself, he needs to surround himself with pastoral staff who will help him take care of the day-to-day duties of hospital visits, counseling, comforting the bereaved, and answering questions that come up during the week.

Often those with pastoral gifts are looked on as less important than the teacher, but their function in the body of Christ is absolutely essential. (We will look at the various gifts in chapter 5.) In the book of Acts, a problem arose because the widows in the church "were being overlooked in the daily distribution of food" (Acts 6:1). The answer was to find men in the church "known to be full of the Spirit and wisdom" (Acts 6:3), to wait on tables and attend to the widows' needs.

The lack of practical service to the poor was causing a serious problem in this multicultural church, and without resolution it would certainly have led to a split. Because of their quick response to the situation, "the word of God spread. The number of disciples in Jerusalem increased rapidly, and a large number of priests became obedient to the faith" (Acts 6:7).

On a recent visit to Angola Prison in Louisiana, once called the bloodiest prison in America, we met a remarkable man—Warden Burl Cain. Under his leadership, this once hopeless place has been transformed into a dynamic and amazing institution. About two thousand of the five thousand prisoners are now Christian men, and eighty are attending a Bible school within the prison. He told us that the secret of his success was something his mom said to him when he became a warden. This committed Christian woman told her son, "You know, *you are responsible* for the souls under your care." This one man, with the power of Christ, took these words to heart and changed what had seemed unchangeable.

As leaders of a church, John and I often tremble at the Scripture that says we must give an account for those under our care (Hebrews 13:17). How frightening to know we will answer for the souls of others! If one man can transform a prison of five thousand, no pastor will be exempt from accounting for the souls under his care, no matter how large his church or busy his schedule may be.

The advantage of a small church is that the pastor is able to know everyone by name and even carry out many of the servant functions in the congregation. If we have a church clean-up day, John is always there with the other men—raking, picking up litter, and bonding with them as they work together. This is probably his most valuable time spent with the men of the congregation.

John and I are convinced that as a whole Christians in our country are over taught—we all know a lot more than we can ever live. Instead of running from conference to conference to hear the latest teaching coming down the pike, we need to learn how to live out what we have already learned. Every time we hear a teaching and do not put it into practice in our lives, our hearts become hardened.

Little by little we grow "Word hardened," until we may have great knowledge and the ability to expound on a variety of biblical topics, but we are not living obedient Christian lives. We are not respecting our boss at work, loving our wife, honoring our husband, caring for the widow and orphan, keeping our minds pure and untainted by the world—all those simple things that Jesus said show we are His disciples. One wife expressed it this way to me: "I know my husband knows a lot more Scripture than I do; he often quotes it to me. He just can't seem to live it."

Religious Zealots or Obedient Disciples?

A lot of us in the church today have become religious zealots, traveling all over the world to hear a personal prophecy, experience the latest revival, hear the newest revelation, or learn the identity of the Antichrist. Yet we have neglected the more important matters of the law—justice, mercy, and faithfulness. We equate our learning with our being and have compared ourselves with a false measure.

> For it is not those who *hear* the law who are righteous in God's sight, but it is those who *obey* the law who will be declared righteous. (Romans 2:13)
> Now that you *know* these things, you will be blessed if you *do* them. (John 13:17)

I am tired of being invited to speak to groups of women who want to be blessed and yet do nothing to bless others with the blessings they have received. We all suffer from spiritual greed to some extent, wanting more knowledge, more blessing, and more revelation. Then, sadly, we take what we have received and put it in our "trophy box" to display and impress others. But Jesus told us that the real blessing is in the *doing*.

In Ezekiel 34, the Lord is chastising the spiritual shepherds of Israel for their neglect of the sheep (the people under their care). He tells them they only take care of themselves and then lists the things they have not done for the sheep: "You have not strengthened the weak or healed the sick or bound up the injured. You have not brought back the strays or searched for the lost" (v. 4).

Each one of these functions involves a very intimate and time-consuming relationship with the sheep. It cannot be accomplished with a forty-five minute sermon on Sunday morning. I am a teacher myself, and I believe God speaks through anointed teaching. I realize that teaching can be very helpful and strengthening, but it must be applied to each sheep personally, and that takes time—a great deal of time.

After the resurrection, when Jesus appeared the third time to the disciples, He asked Peter three times, "Simon son of John, do you truly love me more than these?" Each time Peter assured the Lord that he loved Him, Jesus said something about feeding and taking care of His sheep/lambs (John 21:15–17). The proof of our love for Jesus is caring for His people. Those who know husbandry tell us that sheep require more care than any other type of livestock. So the picture painted here is very appropriate. Those of us who are serving as shepherds/leaders for God's kids know how difficult the job is at times!

I love putting together a teaching. I sit alone and study in quiet and solitude. It is a peaceful time with the Lord and also very fulfilling when I see the end product. On the other hand, giving hands-on care to people can be a frustrating experience. Many times John and I have put lots of time and money into certain individuals only to have them leave when they saw what they believed was a greener pasture somewhere else.

If the American church is going to thrive, we must change from a predominately teaching model to one that includes shepherding. Teachers are essential to teach sound doctrine, but we also need shepherd leaders to impact our culture today. "The future of the Church largely depends upon the emergence of leaders—not necessarily seminary graduates, pastors, or professional clergy, but individuals called by God to lead—who will commit their lives to the Church and cast God's vision for ministry without flinching. These anointed ones will motivate people to get involved, and lead the way in amassing the resources necessary to complete the required tasks."[4]

We knew John was called to lead this fellowship of believers, but we were soon overwhelmed with the needs of the people while trying to fulfill God's vision for us as a congregation. Since John worked as a dentist forty hours a week, we found we were both overworked and growing "weary in doing good" (Galatians 6:9). Thank goodness, God had already supplied an answer to our predicament.

Applying the Lessons

- *Take steps to ensure that your leader can preach and teach without being constrained by financial or size concerns.*

- *Build networks for "at risk" church members, and look at other mentor programs to help people walk out what they are being taught from the Bible.*

- *Make sure that there are enough shepherding pastors to take care of the day-to-day needs of the people under your church's care.*

Bible Study

As I sit in my comfortable chair and
gaze at the faces I am instructing,
I wonder if
I am only producing others
who will also sit in comfortable chairs
and share His teachings.

His teachings
can only be understood by living,
not by numerous words
savored with coffee
and soon forgotten
at the bottom of the cup.

His teachings
took place in open-air classrooms,
or standing-room-only indoors,
with miracles to prove a point,
forgiveness, for instance.

One day a man had friends
who cared enough to leave
their comfortable chairs
and work their way through the crowds,
determined he would be healed.

They found a way to lower him into
the very presence of the One
who lived all things He taught,
and the man was healed
because they heard the Word
and *did* something.

Save us from the delusion that
the hearing is the doing,

THE SHEPHERD AS LEADER • 57

or we grow in holiness according
to accumulated knowledge
of Your Word.

    Make us understand
every Word heard and not lived
is a judge,
standing at the door, convicting us,
deciding our destiny
as we sit in our comfortable chairs.

Functioning As a Body

We have different gifts, according to the grace given us.
ROMANS 12:6

The answer to our dilemma of being overworked came through listening to a tape study by Bob Mumford on house churches. Consisting of twelve people each, these groups met together weekly to encourage, exhort, and hold each other accountable to their Christian commitment.

Today, a number of churches have tried small groups, cell groups, house churches, or whatever name they use, but thirty years ago we had little information on them and few models to emulate. It is interesting that even with such a variety of models to consider small groups have never caught on in most churches; according to recent Barna statistics, "Fewer than one out of every five adults is presently active in one."[1] This is an unfortunate statistic since most personal growth in Christianity takes place in a small, intimate group structure.

We decided that we did not want our house church experience to be a miniature church service or a Bible study. We wanted it to be a place where a person could be transparent and vulnerable and learn how to live out the gospel, where the knowledge they had received from wonderful teachings could be applied to their everyday lives.

The problem with some of the other models (Bible study groups, worship groups, or teaching/discussion groups) is that they mimic the "spectator mode" of the larger church. Often they cannot, because of their structure, foster deep relationships that result in the person understanding his or her place in the body of Christ. This understanding can come only through vulnerability and openness among the members of a house church. It is so important for each person attending to feel the freedom to share with one another.

THE IMPORTANCE OF UNDERSTANDING SPIRITUAL GIFTS

Some years ago I was asked to do a retreat for the women of another church that was large and also had small groups in place. The night before the retreat I met with the wives of the leaders of these small groups. A friend I brought with me shared what her experience had been in our house church.

In her testimony she shared that her husband was the pastor of a small church and a dynamic, prophetic man. She, however, felt she had no role in their church. A main source of conflict between them was the church's counseling ministry. She felt that she had good insight into the women's lives and also had a desire to help them. But the church model they followed only allowed for the pastor to provide counseling for the congregation.

When she and her pastor husband joined our house church, they began to understand their differing gifts. For the first time, they saw how their spiritual gifts complemented each other. As often happens, they were polar opposites in their motivational gifts. A motivational gift is the basic inward drive that God places in each Christian to express His love. The husband was prophetic, and his wife was a mercy giver.

In the house church setting, her husband was able to see how she balanced his "tell it like it is" style. She showed keen discernment in our house church as she shared with the other members.

Her honesty and vulnerability were refreshing and caused other women in the house church to open up and share. As he watched this happen, her husband realized that she was quite capable of counseling with the women in his church, and by turning some of it over to her, he would have more free time to become involved in the community. She told the leaders' wives in the larger church that she and her husband now saw themselves as a team, which gave them a new zeal and unity in their calling.

The next day the women who heard her went to the pastor of their church and told him they wanted to see their house churches structured after our model. The pastor called John and asked if he could visit us and study the makeup of our house churches. After several days with us, he concluded that he couldn't follow our model because he wanted the designated leader to have total control of the house church.

"Your house churches give too much freedom to individuals to share and counsel," he told us. "I want to retain control over our house churches, to make sure they don't get out of hand."

We have heard this again and again over the years. Most pastors feel that the members of the church are unqualified to give advice and guide one another. It is safer to have a discussion group centered on a Bible study where the leader couple is firmly in control.

We do choose our house church leader couples carefully, but we usually do not select people who would dominate and control the house church. This type of leader would defeat our goal, which is to involve every person. Our main focus is that the leader couple are people of godly character and integrity who love and care for the people of God. We need couples that have God's wisdom for the practical issues of life and have demonstrated this by their own lives.

RELEASING MINISTRY TO THE BODY OF CHRIST

The question that frequently comes up when people learn about our house church is what qualifies the people in a house church to counsel one another? In our psychological age, even the church is hooked on sending people out from the church for counseling rather than counseling one another from within the congregation. There are, of course, times when people need professional counseling, but it should always be administered within a Christian framework and in the power of the Holy Spirit.

When we first began to structure house churches, all of our leaders studied an excellent book by Jay E. Adams called *Competent to Counsel.* One of the things he said that really struck a chord with us was how we must put Christ at the center of all our attempts to counsel one another. "Jesus Christ is at the center of all true Christian counseling. Any counseling which moves Christ from that position of centrality has to the extent it has done so ceased to be Christian."[2]

Adams believes that the kind of counseling done within Christian circles should be *nouthetic* counseling (taken from the Greek word *noutheteo,* which means to admonish, warn, and instruct). The premise of the book is "According to Paul, all Christians must teach and confront one another in a *nouthetic fashion.*"[3] He points out that in both Romans 15:14 and Colossians 3:16 Paul urges Christians to "confront one another nouthetically."[4] This type of activity is presented by Paul as a normal, everyday activity, something that is a natural part of the Christian body life.

Since every member of the body of Christ is indwelt by the Holy Spirit of God and has been given spiritual gifts, each person has something to contribute. Granted, some Christians are still immature in their spiritual knowledge and operation of their gifts. But that doesn't mean they will stay that way. One of the purposes of house church is to help each person understand his motivational gift and grow in the knowledge of Christ so that in time he too can minister to other believers in a nouthetic way.

Our house churches provide a setting where believers can develop a deeper relationship with Jesus Christ. They also serve as a training ground for developing leaders and a place for inner healing and ministry. In the smaller setting of a house church people have the opportunity to develop godly character and grow spiritually as they share their life in Christ with others. Character development requires accountability and house church provides plenty of that; we hold each other accountable to "walk out" the problems in our lives according to biblical principles.

Many Christians are unwilling to be held accountable—they still live in the "just Jesus and me" mindset. But God has placed us in a body so that we cannot fulfill

> **God has placed us in a body so that we cannot fulfill our destiny apart from each other.**

our destiny apart from each other. Being in a body does not mean sitting in a church, hearing a teaching, and going home to do my own thing. It means being intimately connected to others in the body, which implies a mutual accountability. Paul's somewhat humorous caricature of the body of Christ in 1 Corinthians 12 mentions that we cannot say to other parts of the body, "I don't need you!" (v. 21).

Personal Responsibility

One thing that we make very clear is that we do not assume the responsibility of another person's spiritual growth. Each member of Christ's body will ultimately answer to God for his or her life. Our counsel or advice is given only as a *recommendation* or possible solution, but all final decisions are to be made by the individual as he or she seeks God's will.

We do not discuss sexual issues in a house church situation. We feel that a private counseling session is more helpful for these kinds of cases. We also have several Christian counseling clinics in our area where we send those who need more than what a house group is qualified to provide.

Before a person joins one of our house church groups we have that person read an "informed consent" form and ask him or her to sign a house church covenant document. Some of the requirements to join are that the person is willing to share laterally with the members of the house church and that he or she agrees to be vulnerable, transparent, and accountable to the other members of the group. Everyone must be willing to deal with fears and have a desire to grow in their motivational and ministry gifts.

Occasionally people sign the "informed consent" form but do

not abide by the rules. They are quick to minister to others in need but are closed to any ministry themselves, or they only come occasionally—when their favorite sports team isn't playing that evening on TV. In these cases we usually ask the person to reconsider his commitment and suggest he might not be ready for the house church format.

The weekly congregational meeting is a wonderful time to come together in corporate praise and worship that prepares us to hear the Word of God. We are instructed to "not neglect our church meetings, as some people do" (Hebrews 10:25 TLB). However, the large meeting is not a place where we can receive personal counsel and encouragement. Many people feel lost in a crowd and in that setting are unable to relate to other members of the body.

Karl Olsson, a pastor and former president of North Park College and Seminary, has said, "The size of the membership has been the measuring stick of the church's power and influence. The effect of organization and bigness has been to conceal the needs of the individual members. By observing an outward conformity to the value system of the church—attending services, paying tithes and offerings, and maintaining moral decorum—the Christian man or woman has been able to hide his or her need for forgiveness, consolation, and encouragement."[5]

Heart to Heart Sharing

I believe that deep down every person seeks intimate relationship with brothers and sisters in the family of God. The house church helps new people plug in quickly and learn how to function as part of a team. It is a place to deal with problems that aren't major. Often the problem that one person shares is common to everyone in the room. I don't know how many times I have been struggling with a difficulty in my life and someone in our house church shares the identical situation. As that person receives counsel I am also receiving hope and encouragement, knowing that I am not alone in my struggle.

As we listen to those with more experience share their personal history and give counsel from the Word of God, we also learn how to counsel. It is wonderful training for future leaders. At the end of a house church meeting, we usually gather around and pray for the person who shared that evening. Often these prayer times turn into a healing or deliverance experience for the person. It edifies and encourages all of us to see a brother or sister set free from a particular bondage.

Recently in our house church, Corine, a former drug addict, shared the grief she was feeling because her mother had passed away before she had the opportunity to see Corine restored and walking with Christ. Corine is now the director of Tabitha House, a residence for women with addictive backgrounds, but she had great sorrow because of the way she had judged her mother. We suggested she write a letter to her mother, expressing her regret about how she had treated her as well as gratitude to the Lord for His deliverance.

The next Sunday evening at house church she brought her letter to read to us. All of us had tears in our eyes as we heard Corine pour out her heart through the letter and seek God's forgiveness. Later, during prayer, the spirit of depression that had hovered over her life was lifted, and she was set free from her grief. This type of intimate sharing and release that Corine experienced is only possible through the intimacy of a small group meeting where people trust each other enough to be honest and vulnerable.

The book of James encourages us to seek out the help of fellow believers. "Confess your sins to each other and pray for each other so that you may be healed" (James 5:16). This is exactly what happened to Corine—she confessed her sins through the letter, and she was forgiven and healed through prayer. Of course, we do not need an intermediary person to receive forgiveness and healing from Jesus. But sometimes it is helpful to have others who will share the experience with us.

I have known people who have struggled with secret sin for years and years, confessing it again and again to God without finding freedom from it. I have also seen that same person, impressed by the Holy Spirit of God to confess that secret sin in house church, find immediate freedom through public confession. We are relational people by nature, and we need relationships with loving brothers and sisters who will assure us of God's forgiveness when we can't forgive ourselves.

The Wednesday after her deliverance from depression, Corine read her letter to the entire church. Many came to the altar that night during worship to release similar judgments on their parents and to be set free from guilt. We find that often house church ministry spills over into the congregational meeting and others beyond the house church are helped by another's experience of freedom. Personal testimony is often the most powerful teaching tool.

This is the type of relationship people are seeking in the church. Some years ago I read the following quote from Karl Olsson and was greatly impacted by his wisdom. "I am not sure, for example, that attending Sunday morning worship in the average church is a primary human need, or that family prayer is the most important thing in keeping a family together, or that getting everybody to read the Bible is going to make the country significantly moral, or that having people join a church is in itself an objective of major consequence. All of these things have value, of course, but are they responses to the deepest human needs?"[6]

In answer to Karl Olsson's penetrating question, I would state from thirty-four years of experience that the deepest need of a Christian is intimate relationships—first with God and second with their brothers and sisters in Christ. Sadly, the traditional church has often failed its members in meeting this need.

"Surveys show that the number-one thing people look for in a church today is fellowship. But what most modern Westerners seek is a far cry from what the Bible describes and what the early church practiced. . . . To some it means the warm, affirming, 'hot-tub' religion that soothes frayed nerves and provides relief from the stresses of everyday life."[7]

This type of "fellowship" is therapeutic but not character building. God's purpose for every one of us in the body of Christ is that we might "be conformed to the likeness of his Son, that he might be the firstborn among many brothers" (Romans 8:29). Being conformed to the likeness of Christ is going to take some blood (His), sweat, and tears (ours). It requires a group of people so committed to one another that they will risk losing a relation-ship in order to speak the truth in love to each other.

Not a New Idea

Many years after we had established our house church format, we discovered that John Wesley, in an attempt to rediscover the vitality of the early church, established meetings called classes that were almost identical to our house churches. "The class meeting encapsulated several of the key principles of New Testament Christianity: personal growth within the context of an intimate fellowship, accountability for spiritual stewardship, 'bearing one another's burdens,' and 'speaking the truth in love.'"[8]

Wesley's class meeting provided a setting for behavioral change. "The 'class meeting' turned out to be the primary means of bringing millions of England's most desperate people into the liberating discipline of Christian faith."[9] Little did we know then that the Holy Spirit was leading us in the same way and for the same purpose.

At the same time we were establishing house churches, we were also learning about the different motivational gifts that are listed in Romans 12.

> We have different gifts, according to the grace given us. If a man's gift is *prophesying*, let him use it in proportion to his faith. If it is *serving*, let him serve; if it is *teaching*, let him teach; if it is *encouraging*, let him encourage; if it is *contributing* to the needs of others, let him give generously; if it is *leadership*, let him govern diligently; if it is *showing mercy*, let him do it cheerfully. (Romans 12:6–8)

In 1980, John and I went to a Bill Gothard Advanced Seminar and learned for the first time about these different motivations. Today, many Christians have taken Bill's original study and have developed it in their own manner. Studies on motivational gifts abound today, but for us at that time it was a defining moment.

I will never forget the impact of hearing Bill teach on these motivations. John and I were spellbound listening to the descrip-tion of the prophetic motivation when Bill ended with this statement: "Men, if your wife is prophetically motivated, you are going to have to listen to her because she has a deep need to express her spiritual perceptions."

John turned to me and with new insight said, "He's talking about you!"

A little later as Bill described the gift of organization, it was my turn to be surprised and humbled when he said, "This is one gift that doesn't appear to be spiritual." Then he added, "But it is!"

Since that enlightening conference I have come to see that John is the perfect pastor for our type of church, and yes, he is spiritual—usually more so than his wife. He describes himself with his organizational gift as an orchestra conductor. He doesn't have to know how to play all the instruments; he just has to know when to call in the brass, the woodwinds, percussion, and others. And this he does very well. So well, in fact, that about 90 percent of the people in our church are involved in using their gift(s) in some sort of ministry.

This discovery freed John from the burden of teaching. He realized that he wasn't called to teach; his calling was to lead and pastor. He developed a teaching team of men and women who were gifted teachers, and this team does most of the teaching in our church. Every six to eight weeks John will "teach" on a Wednesday evening, but he mainly shares his vision for the church, which gives great encouragement to the congregation.

THE GIFTS AT WORK

As we began to learn more about the various motivations, we found that in every one of our house church meetings of twelve to fourteen people, most, if not all, of the gifts were represented. A motivational gift is the *basic inward drive that God places in each Christian to express His love*. It is the passion that drives everything else we do. As we taught our people about the gifts, we began to experience and recognize the flow of these different motivations in our Sunday night house church meetings.

Here's how it might work. Someone shares that he's having a problem at work with his boss. The person with a prophetic motivational gift—the "prophet"—would point out that his boss might remind him of his father, and maybe he had judged his father or still had deep resentment toward him, and that was affecting his relationship with his boss. As we explored this possibility, other motivational gifts would come into the mix. The "teacher" might share a Scripture, telling the man he should work as if he were working for God, or honor his boss as certain verses instruct. The "mercy giver" would try to pour oil on any wounds he felt were inflicted by the prophet. The "exhorter" would encourage the man in his situation, perhaps by sharing a similar story from his own life. The person with the gift of giving might suggest he look for another job, volunteering to help him out financially until he can find a new position. And the person with the gift of serving would make sure that his coffee cup was refilled.

This might sound like a confusing situation, but an amazing thing happens as you watch the different gifts flow in a meeting. All at once you recognize *the voice of God* speaking through one of the people. Usually everything said will be valuable, but one person will have *the* answer, the advice coming straight from the Holy Spirit. It might be the exhorter, the mercy giver, or the teacher, but we would all agree . . . that's it!

It is wonderful, even supernatural, to watch God's people minister to one another in their gifting. This is how we learn to recognize another's gift, seeing how they minister to others time after time.

Misuse of Our Gifts

Of course there are times when a person misuses his gift, but in our experience this has been rather infrequent. Most people need encouragement to speak up. Few have to be encouraged to be quiet. We often will ask the shy members of the group what they are thinking, and it is amazing to see that they usually have a well-defined opinion based on their gift but were too timid to share it with the group.

When we do have this problem, it is usually easily discerned that the person is contributing to the discussion from his flesh or from a secular philosophy and is going cross current. The house church leader or another member will turn the ministry to the person who made the inappropriate remark with a question like: "Don't you think that remark reveals an unresolved issue in your life?" Often deep ministry results from this type of exchange.

It is no wonder that we see the most growth in a person's spiritual life taking place in the house church situation. It is here that he can be real and release the gifts God has put within him. Here he can also admit his fears and weaknesses without being judged.

John Wesley believed that the small group was the *primary* way a person grew in his relationship with God. His confidence was summed up in this comment: "I have found by experience that one of these [people] has learned more from one hour's close discourse than ten years' public preaching."[10] In fact, historians believe it was the small groups that accounted for the success of Wesley, while the fruit of many of his contemporary evangelists died with them.

If the basic need of every Christian is to have meaningful relationships, then the church must form a strategy to meet this need. If we don't, we stand to lose precious fruit. Understanding the motivational gifting of each person and giving that person a venue in which he can use and understand his gift is key to fulfilling Christ's pronouncement to "feed my sheep."

Applying the Lessons

- *Spend some time researching which small group model would best meet the relational needs of your particular congregation.*

- *Search your own heart to determine how much you trust the Holy Spirit to guide the members of your church. If you can't release the control of meetings to anyone but yourself, ask others you trust to pray with you about this issue.*

- *Look for ways you can release other believers into places of service according to their motivational gift and spiritual passion. Encourage wider participation by moving away from the spectator approach to services.*

The Body

Who placed me here
in this unpresentable part
of the body?
And next to members
I would never choose,
had I been given any choice.

There's the rub!
I never had any choice!
He never asked me if
I would like to spend my life unnoticed,
among equally anonymous members.
He made the decision as
He makes all decisions,
and I either agree with Him or
live in constant contention.

"Why?" I asked.
No, yelled, in my ignorance.
"Why can't I
help with the planning?"
Quietly, through my thoughts,
He replied,
because I have the blueprint.

What About the Kids?

Let the little children come to me, and do not hinder them, for the kingdom of God belongs to such as these.
LUKE 18:16

When God intervened in our lives, John and I were attending the local Catholic church. In the ten years that we had been members of that church no one ever asked us to help out teaching catechism. But only three months after we were born again, the secretary of our local Catholic church called to ask us if we would consider doing a class for high-school juniors in our home.

We knew this opportunity was from God, and we only had one question: "Can we use the Bible as our textbook for the class?"

"Of course," replied the secretary. "Each couple may choose their own format for the course."

We felt led to ask the secretary if they needed more teachers, and she said they did. So we suggested a couple who were close friends of ours and who had recently been born again and filled with the Holy Spirit. Incredibly, they were also assigned a class—the sophomores. They planned to use the Bible as their text too.

Here we were, babes in Christ, only six months old, and already we had a group of seventeen high-school juniors coming to our home every week to listen to us tell them about Jesus. Of course, most of them came because of the threats and pressure of their parents, but we didn't care—we had a captive audience.

Each week we shared the ongoing testimony of our conversion and studied the Scriptures about being born again. God was present in a powerful way, bringing revelation and sometimes even miracles of physical healing and deliverance.

Over the course of the nine months, every one of those seventeen young people gave their life to Christ. Each one was born again and filled with the Holy Spirit. The last one to surrender was a young man named Joe, who was deeply involved in Satanism. He had witnessed many miraculous manifestations of the power of God as he attended our class, but he was afraid to reject Satanism because he was sure something terrible would happen to him if he did.

One night John and I were sitting in a Denny's restaurant having coffee with Joe and a friend of his, and suddenly the Holy Spirit seemed to fall on us and surround our table. Joe looked at us with tears in his eyes and said he wanted to give his life to Christ.

We quickly drove home to pray with him, and then he brought all his occult literature and paraphernalia to be burned. What a wonderful bonfire we had that night; the word quickly spread among the teens that the last sheep had come into the fold.

Our friends had similar victories with the sophomores that were meeting in their home. Often we got the two groups together for prayer and Bible study. These young people formed the core of our early church and were the most fervent evangelists we have ever known.

We were a relatively youthful church, with many teens, young adults, and a few couples like us—in their thirties with children. Those early years were filled with a number of delightful wedding celebrations as these young people married. It wasn't long before we realized we had quite a few small children in the church and many were asking: *What about the kids?*

We had our Wednesday evening service, Sunday night house church, and Tuesday night Bible study, but there was nothing planned for the children. As we were desperately searching for ideas, I remembered hearing somewhere that long after a child forgets what he *learned* in Sunday school, he will remember how he *felt*! Children relate to the world primarily through their feelings, and we knew this was the key to reaching their hearts for Christ. But how would we do it?

Most research indicates that if children do not make a decision for Christ before they leave home at about age eighteen, the majority will not become Christians. These early years are when the Christian message has the most impact on people. Yet for many children, what they were exposed to in Sunday school didn't connect with their lives in any way. The material was often boring, dreary, and less than motivating.

ENVISIONING A DYNAMIC KIDS CHURCH

I remember my children sitting through long and, to them, boring sermons, pestering me every five minutes to go home. Church wasn't a very exciting place for them, and they certainly didn't feel good about being there. So we set a goal to establish a church for children within Spirit of God Fellowship that would be so exciting and relevant to them that, even as adults, their feelings about Christianity would still be positive. That is how "Kids Church" was birthed.

For several years we struggled along, trying to present interesting skits and puppet shows once a month for our kids on Sunday morning. Those of us participating in the production were rank amateurs and unfortunately had long ago forgotten what it felt like to be a kid. But even during our early years, when we keenly felt our inexperience, our children responded positively to our efforts, asking that we meet every other week rather than only once a month. Their spirits were hungry to be fed even though the meal was less than sumptuous.

We limped along in a hit-or-miss fashion until our son Tom graduated from college in 1988 and returned home. He turned out to be God's answer to our ambitious goal, truly a miraculous provision that only became clear to us as things unfolded.

I am always amazed at the process of seeing a vision become reality. First, God births a vision in us, and then we work very hard to bring that vision about *in our own strength*. After falling on our face a few times, we are finally ready to call on Him. Then if the vision is truly from God, He will bring it to fruition in His own time and way.

When we came to that point with our Kids Church, God brought Tom into the picture. But I'll let Tom tell you his own story.

GOD'S INTERVENTION

Halfway through college and a thousand moral miles from my Christian upbringing, I knew I needed a change to escape my self-centered lifestyle. So in 1985, I took a year off, moved to Texas, and joined Youth With A Mission, a Christian discipleship-training ministry.

The first three months of the training we lived on a ranch, where we prayed, heard teachings, received counsel, and worked all of the jobs necessary to keep the ranch operating. The next three months were spent in Mexico City doing outreach to the poor, the homeless, and the children. There were so many children there, some without shoes, and many without parents.

Because I spoke enough Spanish to communicate with the people and had previous acting experience, I spent most of my time on stage performing in a show designed to present the gospel message to children. Often we would drive all over the city, performing two or three times a day. Hundreds of children and even some adults gave their lives to Christ at the end of each show. This was an exciting experience, and I learned a lot about effectively reaching children with the gospel.

The next year I returned to college and put my experience in Mexico City behind me so I could focus on finishing my studies and graduating. Even though I thought my time in Mexico was an isolated experience that would have no bearing on the rest of my life, God was setting in motion the groundwork for His next vision for Spirit of God Fellowship.

God gave my parents a vision for a new form of children's ministry, but there was no one with the experience or training to bring that vision to reality. However, as the church had seen so many times in the past, when God births a vision, we need to step out in faith and trust Him to take care of the details—little things like *how in the world are we going to do this?*

Some women in the church made puppets, the men made a puppet stage, and people with absolutely no experience set out to do two shows a month. Because our main service is on Wednesday night, the first and third Sunday of each month were set aside for "Kids Church." The various house churches took turns with the responsibility of putting on a show.

In a university a hundred miles away, I was blissfully unaware of how my path would intersect with theirs in God's timing. I was busy writing hundreds of poems, stories, and short plays, all of a serious and philosophical nature. I loved to write and knew that I had some talent for it as well as a lot of creativity. At that time I wanted to be intellectual and deep, to provoke thought and reflection in the reader. Many of my writings were dark and metaphorical, because this is how I thought my talent could best be used. Little did I know what God was preparing for me.

After graduation I moved back home and began attending the church again. There were many changes that had taken place while I was gone, but the one that really got my attention was the children's ministry. Maybe it was the memories of my time in Mexico, or the lackluster shows that were presented. Whatever the reason, I started to give it a lot of thought.

I knew the days were gone when children would be satisfied with a flannel board presentation and a snack. Children were growing up with TV cartoons, video games, computers, Game Boys, MTV, etc. As a result of being entertained by these mind-stimulating activities, I knew they suffered from extremely short attention spans.

Being young, idealistic, and outspoken, I was quick to point out to my father that the Kids Church program was unprofessional, disorganized—and boring. Brimming with my newly acquired knowledge and experience, I told him that the church, in spite of its good intentions, had no clue about how to effectively reach children and teach them in a sustainable way. I also pointed out their Sunday school was an activity geared primarily for the children of churched people, and I had some ideas about how to make it more evangelical.

I was all tact . . . but God was letting my ego set me up. The mantra of our church is "If you think you can do it better, then stop talking about it and get in there and help." Not surprisingly, my father responded to my remarks by challenging me to get involved. I was quick to accept the challenge because I had no idea what God was doing.

Initially I made a three-month commitment to help out in the children's ministry. My idea was that I would work with each small group when it was their turn to put on the program so that we could achieve some continuity and learn from our successes and mistakes. My role would be to stay in the background and be the facilitator.

I did not plan on acting or being visible at all during the programs. I wanted no recognition or praise from the church. Much of this came from a false humility, a fear of failure, and probably more than anything, an unwillingness to be identified with children's theater. After all, *my plans* for my talent focused on serious, challenging projects that would best convey my intellectual, insightful, and brilliant persona. In retrospect, I may have been a little full of myself. No, let me change that. I *was* full of myself, not a *little*, but *a lot*. Fortunately, God was gracious to gently lead me in spite of my arrogance. Had I insisted on clinging to my own ideas, I would have missed out on all the wonderful plans He had for our children's ministry.

Guiding Our Steps

My original plan lasted exactly one show. I found it difficult and unproductive to work with a small group of people who were participating out of a need but not necessarily because they felt called to be a part of it. So I had to revamp my approach to better suit the circumstances. My new vision was to assemble a *permanent* group of actors, prop people, sound technicians, and writers to commit to the vision and ministry. I still only gave myself three months to do all this.

A small group of people volunteered to be a part of the Kids Church ministry, and I was initially excited. But soon it became clear that they had no discernable experience, talent, or applicable skills for the task. Another problem: Several of them claimed instant nausea every time they got on stage. *Oh boy*, I thought. *This is going to be fun.* My greatest consolation through this transition stage was that this was God's ministry, not mine. So these were ultimately His problems to work out.

My commitment of three months was, as you might guess, extended quite a bit under God's direction. Fifteen years later and a world away from those early days of struggle, failures, rehearsals running past midnight, and weekly panic attacks, God has built an amazing ministry through us. We try to keep the shows exciting and fast-moving because the new generation of children (born between 1984 and 2003) is an entirely new breed. These kids present a radical departure from traditional Western thought. Their way of thinking is so different from other generations that it's like comparing a modern man to one from medieval times.

Today we have more than forty people involved in writing, acting, props, costumes, lighting, sound, video, and merchandising. We perform eighteen original shows each season—September through May—and incorporate skits, songs, puppets, pantomime, and PowerPoint presentations. Each show teaches a basic biblical principle, and we often act out parables and stories from the Old and New Testaments as well as situations showing how the principle can be applied in our lives today.

Unexpected Results

More than three hundred children and adults regularly attend these shows. Many of these are visitors. Kids Church has inadvertently become a tremendous outreach in the community. Surprisingly, many unchurched adults want their children to be exposed to the gospel, and Kids Church is a non-threatening way for this to happen.

There have been some unexpected directions the Kids Church program has taken us. We had many visitors from other churches visit us in the early days of Kids Church, who heard about our program and wanted to start something similar in their own churches.

It was our intent from the beginning to share our unique and effective program with anyone who asked. We knew that it would not be God's desire for us to be proud and guarded, trying to "pro-tect" our program in order to keep the bragging rights of a suc-cessful ministry. There's no way He would have continued to bless us with that kind of attitude.

When visitors came we would give them a tour of our facility, sit down and talk with them about how we began, answer their questions, and then offer to help them in any way we could. This help might include giving them some of our scripts, videos of shows we had done, puppet patterns, puppet stage blueprints—in short, anything that might help them get started. As they were leaving we also gave them our phone number so they could call any time for assistance or guidance in developing their own children's program.

When the visitors returned to their own churches, filled with excitement about starting a program, in almost every case the pas-tor and/or elders would turn a deaf ear to the idea of bringing something new into their church. When these people asked their pastors to watch the videos of our program to get an understand-ing of what we were doing, they seldom did. We didn't know what to suggest when everything got stalled at their end.

One day we got a call from a woman who had visited us and gone back to her church excited and eager to begin a similar min-istry. She told us what we had heard so often: "I just can't get my pastor to understand what I want to do. I'm sure if I could get him to *see it*, he would be excited about it too. Do you have a 'road show' that could come to our church and put on a performance?"

I was about to tell her, "Sorry, we can't help you there," because we didn't have a traveling road show. But somehow, when I opened my mouth to speak, I found myself saying, "Sure, when do you want us to come?"

I still remember the looks on the faces of our actors and tech-nicians at the next meeting when I told them we had one month to put together a traveling version of our program, including a portable stage, sound system, and new scripts. Apparently God had gone before me, because after explaining that this was perhaps God's next step in our ministry, their reaction was excitement and a willingness to put even more hours into the work.

One month later we performed our first road show for the

congregation of the aforementioned woman who had asked us to come. Afterward, she was given the green light to start a similar ministry of her own. But a few weeks later she called again. "Okay, I have volunteers, and the church has given me funds to get started, but I have no idea what I am doing. Do you have a group that can come and do a full day of training to teach us the basics?"

In response, we put together a group that could do a basic training seminar. Since that time, we have had the opportunity to train many churches. That first church we worked with developed a children's program, and twelve years later it is still going strong.

We have never required a fee or payment of any kind to perform our road show or provide training. If a church asks about payment, we suggest a donation, but we would never refuse to help on the basis of money. The Scripture is plain: "Freely you have received, freely give" (Matthew 10:8). We have performed in orphanages, retirement homes, and even outdoors in town parks.

A church will often take our basic program and fit it to their particular church structure. Most have a Sunday program with the kids while moms and dads listen to the sermon. Often just seeing our program stimulates their creative juices, and they come up with their own brand of church for kids.

Our Kids Church program is seen on the local cable stations of several surrounding towns, and we have been told that it has generated more positive calls than any other show they air. We have grown from a ministry created primarily to teach our children into a successful outreach to both churched and unchurched families. Helping other churches begin their own ministry and reaching into surrounding communities through cable TV are bonuses that God has thrown in. Under His direction, the vision just keeps expanding and improving with time. *(end of Tom's story)*

Recent Developments

In the last several years, Barb Whitlock has stepped up to take over the directorship for our children's ministry. She has brought in some exciting innovations—black light shows, original musicals written by John Russell, a talented Kids Church writer, etc. All this from someone who is a lawyer by day. She has also done a number of video presentations to music involving the kids in the church. The kids love these videos because they are the stars.

Barb realized that the greatest ongoing struggle is to keep Kids Church from becoming pure entertainment and thereby lose the dynamic of ministering to the children's spirits. As a result, efforts have been made to focus on topics that help children in their relationship with God, such as hearing God's voice and knowing the Holy Spirit.

Children are so open to God. The ways we can reach them are limited only by our own lack of imagination. When we win a child we also impact his or her parents. And when we influence a child we also affect future generations. Theodore Roosevelt (1859–1919), our twenty-sixth president, stated this so eloquently:

> All of us who give service, and stand ready for sacrifice, are torch-bearers. We run with the torches until we fall, content if we can then pass them to the hands of some other runners.

There are so many ways to pass the torch on to the next generation through children's ministry. It is a well-known fact that the percentage of Bible-based believers has been steadily decreasing. It is distressing to think that only "four percent (projected) of . . . millennials (born after 1977) are or will be evangelical."[1] We don't have to think of *big* ministries to turn this around. God blesses our smallest efforts in reaching out to those He puts in our path.

A Mexican family moved in next door to a single woman in our church, Barb VanKuiken. One day when Barb was mowing the lawn, the children asked if they could help. Slowly a friendship developed through playing games with the children.

When they found out she was a teacher, they asked if she would give them some help with homework. The parents were very grateful for her tutoring, since they spoke little English and were unable to assist their children with the lessons. Barb has had the opportunity to plant seeds in this family and was even invited to attend the confirmation of their son.

There is probably nothing closer to the heart of God than serving children. They may forget the things they were taught, but they'll remember the kindness and love of those who took time for them. God has moved us far beyond our sincere but inept beginnings as we have continued to give Him the glory and credit through it all. We certainly do not have a monopoly on creativity and talent; there are groups we have worked with that do many things with greater skill.

The important thing is to be faithful to the vision God gives us. Each church will give an account to Him for what they have done with the incredible resources and opportunities they have. Impact-

> They may forget the things they were taught, but they'll remember the kindness and love of those who took time for them.

ing the next generation with the life-changing gospel message is worth our time and effort. The difference we make in our community may not be evident immediately. But that is okay; we can wait for our reward. It's all His work anyway—we are just His servants fleshing out the vision He has birthed in us. So all the glory goes to Him!

Applying the Lessons

- *Take an honest look at your current children's ministry and ask God to show you how it compares to* His *plans for that area of your church.*

- *With your current church staff talk about how you can more effectively present the gospel to both church kids and kids who are unreached in your community.*

- *If your particular style of doing children's ministry is working well, consider how you might share it with other churches in your area.*

Alabaster Jar

I carry you entombed in sinful flesh.
I hide your glory, and
keep it from penetrating
the night beyond.

Though you want to touch the world,
your light is hidden.
Flesh veils it, revealing
pettiness, irritability, and
a greedy, impatient spirit.

The candle you lit in my spirit
has only illuminated my darkness.
Help me to die
to this suffocating flesh,
to release your light
from its dark prison.

So those groping in darkness
might catch a glimpse
of the treasure that resides
in this very earthen vessel.

The Call to Prayer

*Prayer is the first thing, the second thing,
the third thing necessary to a minister. Pray,
then, my dear brother; pray, pray, pray.*
EDWARD PAYSON

*And pray in the Spirit on all occasions with
all kinds of prayers and requests.*
EPHESIANS 6:18

It took about eight years from our small beginnings
to come to a place where we had pretty much settled our church
structure. We felt that we had "arrived" since we even had something for the kids. We were a small community of believers who
loved God and loved each other. We believed we had it all—till
one Wednesday evening.

A man who worked with inner-city gangs came to speak at our
service that night. I don't remember who recommended him, and
we have never seen him again. But God used him to impart a
dynamic word into our church.

He was a rough, plain-looking man dressed in a casual plaid
shirt and blue jeans. As he walked up to the platform to speak, I
remember thinking that with his tousled hair and laid back attitude he wasn't very impressive. I guess I wasn't expecting much
and even wondered why we had invited him to speak.

He wasn't a polished speaker, but from his very first word it was evident that the Holy Spirit spoke through him. We expected a testimony about his life and work with inner-city gangs. Instead, we received a rebuke from God. He spoke on the importance of prayer both in the life of an individual believer and the church as a whole. From time to time throughout his talk he would pause and say, "If this church doesn't get serious about prayer, you will not be here next year!"

We were stunned, because the words came with the conviction of the Holy Spirit. All of us received it as a warning directly from God. I don't think our speaker was even aware of the impact of his words. They weren't delivered in a "thus saith the Lord" style. He spoke simply, in a soft, even hesitant voice, but none of us missed the anointing of God on his message. As he finished, he said again, "If this church doesn't get serious about prayer, you will not be here next year."

It wasn't that we didn't pray, but most of our prayers were centered around our own petty needs and wants. None of us had really spent time in intercessory prayer. Our congregation was something like the people Hugh Price Hughes (1847–1902), a Welsh poet, wrote about in his story *City of Everywhere*:

> A man arrived in a city one cold morning. As he got off the train, the station was like any other station with the crowds and redcaps, except that everybody was barefooted. They wore no shoes. He noticed the cab driver was barefooted. "Pardon me," he asked the driver, "I was just wondering why you don't wear shoes. Don't you believe in shoes?"
>
> "Sure we do," said the driver.
>
> "Why don't you wear them?"
>
> "Ah, that's the question," came the reply. "Why don't we wear shoes? Why don't we?"
>
> At the hotel it was the same. The clerk, bellboys, everybody was barefooted. In the coffee shop he noticed a nice-looking fellow at a table opposite him who was also barefooted. He said, "I notice you aren't wearing any shoes. I wonder why? Don't you know about shoes?"
>
> The man replied, "Of course I know about shoes."
>
> "Then why don't you wear them?"

"Ah, that's the question. Why don't we? Why don't we?"

After breakfast he walked out on the street in the snow but every person he saw was barefooted. He asked another man about it, and pointed out how shoes protect the feet from cold. The man said, "We know about shoes. See that building yonder? That is a shoe factory. We are proud of that plant and every week we gather there to hear the man in charge tell about shoes and how wonderful they are."

"Then why don't you wear shoes?"

"Ah, that's the question."

Of course we believed in prayer. We heard sermons about prayer, we were exhorted to pray and some of us did from time to time. Why didn't we pray—ah, that was the question. Why didn't we?

Our core group of believers met several days later to discuss this very question. We were all convinced that God had spoken to us, but what were we to do? We decided to begin intercessory prayer groups, each led by an elder and his wife. Anyone who wanted to pray for the church and community was invited. These groups were the catalyst and formed the foundation that later birthed our numerous prayer walks and community prayer meetings.

PLANS FOR OUR COMMUNITY

Several years later Carol Gill, a woman in our church with a gift of intercession, read John Dawson's book *Taking Our Cities for God*.[1] Excited by the concept of his book, she spent a day in the local library studying the background of our community as a springboard for prayer. She also made copies of the map of our town and asked for intercessors to pray for certain areas. At that time we prayed for our entire community through intercessory groups.

Five years later she had a more sophisticated plan in place to pray for every home. She had a large village map made up and intercessors signed up for a specific block. They were asked to walk each block and pray in front of every house. Once in a while, a homeowner would come out to see what we were doing. No one was ever offended; in fact, some stayed and joined with us in prayer.

We learned to wait on the Spirit of God to give us a specific word concerning each home so that we could pray in accordance with His will for the residents. It was a great training time for intercessors. After they completed prayer for each home on their block, they colored in the area on the map and signed up for a new block. In this way, we covered every home in our village. Even today, when Carol hears there is a problem on a certain block, she will park on that block and pray specifically for that home.

We were coming to the realization that *God had plans for our community*, and our church was just one small part of that plan. Too often churches become caught up with praying only for their congregation and its programs. But we sensed God was calling us to intercede for every church, every public employee, and every home in South Holland. Our fervent prayer was that God would make South Holland a "city on a hill" that "cannot be hidden" (Matthew 5:14). At the time we had no idea what that meant or why God led us to pray that particular way. But now after fifteen years of intercessory prayer, we are beginning to see the fruit that comes from persisting in prayer.

Just recently one of our state senators, who is also the minister of a very large African-American church in Chicago, spoke at our annual Labor Day praise gathering in South Holland. He mentioned that he has traveled all over the world, and then named many of the cities that he visited: Paris, Rome, Florence, London, and many more. Then he added, "But my very favorite city in the whole world is South Holland! I love this city so much that I bought a home for my parents here."

Those of us who have interceded for so many years were thrilled to hear that. We know that God is bringing about His plan for our city, but we also know the cost of commitment. The two prayer campaigns for our village were just the beginning of what God wanted our church to do.

Hands Across the Village

My husband has a habit of filling his patients' mouths with rolls of cotton and then asking them questions about Christianity. He has even learned how to interpret their *ahs* and grunts into understandable language. Of course, the patient is usually frustrated by the one-sided conversation.

One day John had just finished a gold crown on a woman. As he removed the last of the cotton from her mouth she couldn't wait to continue their conversation, now with intelligible words. They had been discussing (at least John had) their mutual desire to see unity and cooperation between the churches in our village. His patient was a devout Christian intercessor in another local church. When John spoke of his vision to start a monthly prayer meeting with representatives from the different churches in the village, she became gripped by the possibilities. The more they talked, the more convinced they were that this idea was from God.

John introduced her to Patrice Kamstra, a woman from our church with a deep love for unity within the body. Together they decided to host a monthly meeting of believers from the South Holland churches. Their mission would be to pray, first for the unity of the churches, and then for blessing on the village and village officials.

One of the reasons John was excited about this new group was his association with an already existing prayer group called "John 17:21." The name is taken from the Scripture where Jesus is praying for unity among His followers:

> My prayer is not for them alone. I pray also for those who will believe in me through their message, *that all of them may be one, Father, just as you are in me and I am in you. May they also be in us so that the world may believe that you have sent me.* (vv. 20–21)

This group, consisting of pastors from various communities, had met together for seven years. While it provided wonderful times of sharing, John was frustrated that their fellowship and prayer never moved beyond the walls of their meeting place. In this new group he saw the potential to reach out into all areas of our village, beginning with the churches. He knew that in order for the world to believe in Jesus, unity had to come first to the people of God.

At this time John was president of the ministerial association in South Holland. So he wrote a letter inviting all churches to send representatives to the first meeting on January 9, 1997. About five turned up at that first meeting, but it was a start. In all we do God always reminds us, "Do not despise this small beginning" (Zechariah 4:10 TLB).

Patrice and her friend named the new group "Hands Across the Village" because of the praying hands pictured on our water tower. This is the eighth year they have been meeting on a monthly basis. They have never had full participation from all the churches, but they usually have representatives from eight different churches.

It's sad that many pastors are only concerned about their tiny piece of real estate; they don't seem to understand that it's not about us, but about building the collective kingdom of God. When God allowed Jerusalem to be defeated and captured by Babylon, He sent them His word through Jeremiah.

> This is the Message from God-of-the-Angel-Armies, Israel's God, to all the exiles I've taken from Jerusalem to Babylon: "Make yourselves at home there and work for the country's welfare. Pray for Babylon's well-being. If things go well for Babylon, things will go well for you" (Jeremiah 29:4, 7 THE MESSAGE).

God wants us to pray for the places where we live, even though we are told in Hebrews 11:13 that we are like "aliens and strangers" on earth. The heroes of faith mentioned in Hebrews 11 were all "longing for a better country—a heavenly one" (v. 16). As believers in Christ we too are looking forward to our true and lasting home, heaven. While we are here on earth, though, God expects us to identify with and pray for the people in our local community, as mentioned in the Jeremiah passage.

The people who gather to pray at Hands Across the Village do not see themselves as important or powerful, but they have held fast to the Scripture "'Not by might nor by power, but by my Spirit,' says the Lord Almighty" (Zechariah 4:6). They realize that they are not mighty people but, in Patrice's words, "We have a mighty *calling.*"

Often one of the members will bring a news clipping to the meeting about a recent crime in the area. They will not only pray for the victims of the crime but also that the criminal will be caught. Many times they have seen criminals apprehended the day after their prayer session. These few but faithful people are making mighty changes in the lives of every resident in our village as they obey God's call to pray for their community.

We have learned not to grow discouraged by the many who refuse to come and join us but to be encouraged by the few who do give their time sacrificially. I recall one weekend when our youth group was going on retreat and their leaders asked our church congregation to fast and pray that God would anoint their time together. Sadly, I didn't fast or even remember to pray for them.

The next Wednesday night at church, the young people shared about the sovereign move of God at their retreat and the many conversions that took place. As I sat there, convicted of my lack of prayer, it seemed the Holy Spirit whispered to me, *You have no part in this blessing because you neglected to pray and fast.* It is a lesson I have never forgotten.

Praying Protection at a Public Event

In 1998, during a time of intercessory prayer, God gave me a vision for uniting the churches in prayer around the village. Since the Fourth of July is a time when we celebrate the birth of this nation, a country founded upon Christian principles, I thought it would be a great time for the churches to stand at every entrance point into the village and pray for a hedge of protection around South Holland.

Just as God designed the earth with a protective layer of atmosphere to sustain plant and animal life, He has also established a "protective layer" around His people. God put a protective hedge

around the nation of Israel, but their failure to walk in righteousness led to His judgment upon them. He describes in Scripture
how He would administer that judgment: "I will take away its
[Israel's] hedge, and it will be destroyed; I will break down its wall,
and it will be trampled" (Isaiah 5:5).

In South Holland we sought to build a hedge around our village by praying at the fourteen gates or entrance points with representatives from churches in the community. Elisabeth Austin,
head of our intercessory team, set out to implement the vision.
She sent out letters to the twenty-seven churches in South Holland, inviting them to participate. A follow-up call was made to
ensure an elder or pastor would be present and to give them their
assigned "gate."

We have met on the Fourth of July at eight in the morning
every year since that first time in 1999. Each year the pastors and
elders are given particular Scriptures and prayers to be declared at
the various gates of our city. Usually eight or nine churches participate. We would like to see all the churches participating, but we
are glad for those who stand with us year by year. We know that
God is less concerned about how many come than the heartfelt
commitment of those who do.

Every year the focus has been on a different aspect of God's
Word as it relates to the church's role in upholding the entire community. Here are the verses and prayer subjects we have used so
far:

- 1999—Isaiah 60:17b–18. We prayed believing God was building walls around the village and these walls were walls of salvation.
- 2000—Isaiah 33:20. We prayed to lay hold of the borders of
  the village both physically and spiritually. We rolled up papers
  printed with Scripture verses, inserted them into stakes, and
  drove them into the ground as we proclaimed God's ownership. (This was adapted with permission from City Bible
  Church, Portland, Oregon; Frank Damazio, pastor.)
- 2001—We prayed Scriptures according to the prayer of Jabez,
  for blessing and to keep us from evil.

- 2002—Matthew 5:14–16. We called on God to make us a "city on a hill" whose light would shine to other communities as well as our own.
- 2003—Psalm 91. We prayed for God's protection and safety and that no harm or disaster would come upon us.
- 2004—Genesis 26:18. We prayed for God to reopen the wells of our forefathers and renew the flow of life-giving spiritual water, especially in the area of racial reconciliation.
- 2005—2 Corinthians 9:8. God has blessed us so that we can bless others in keeping with the godly heritage of our early settlers.

July 4, 2005, we had two hundred people meet to pray! At our "gate" we had four new village residents join us. They saw our full-page ad in the local paper and were excited to be able to pray for their village. In fact, when we finished praying, one of the women turned to me and said, "We need to do more of this type of prayer." I was able to tell her about our monthly village meeting and encourage her to come.

We have had a number of miraculous reports of God's protection in our village since we began to pray in this way. A South Holland policeman, who is a member of our church, reported that they were chasing a car with two men who had just robbed a bank. As soon as the car entered the "gates" of South Holland the men pulled over and surrendered to police.

MAKING A DIFFERENCE

So often people complain about their communities but never do anything constructive to turn things around. As the people of God, we have been called to serve our cities in both practical and spiritual ways. We encourage our church members to run for local offices. In the last election, seven of our people won seats in government. These positions included a village trustee, a township office, and seats on school and library boards.

However, we sometimes forget that prayer is also a way to be a servant to our communities. The old adage "Prayer changes things" is certainly true. All our community involvement will be worthless if it is not covered by prayer. We may be *God's ground force* in our community, but if we don't prepare beforehand by seeking His face in prayer, we may not take the ground. When we prayed for every person running for office in our village, we saw seven out of eight win their place.

> **All our community involvement will be worthless if it is not covered by prayer.**

When we respond to the command of God to pray for peace and prosperity for our cities, we are serving our neighbors in ways they may never see. But God sees our secret petitions and says He will reward us openly (Matthew 6:6) both by blessing our churches and by granting peace and security to others in our community.

I often think of that man God used to warn our church about our prayerlessness. I shudder to think what would have happened if he hadn't had the boldness to speak God's word to us, or if we had not heeded his word of warning.

We have many intercessory groups functioning in our church today. We do prayer walks in neighborhoods, around schools, and wherever we hear of a need. Three years ago we began to have one of our house churches fast on a rotational basis every day from Monday through Friday, and then meet for prayer. We are not praying twenty-four hours a day as some churches are, but by the grace of God we have become a praying people.

Prayerlessness is a sign of an independent spirit, the conviction that we can manage just fine without God, trusting in our own wisdom and programs. Repentance is the only way to break the grip of this deception, acknowledging our great need for Him in every area of our lives. In return, God will grant us new visions of how prayer can transform our congregations and villages. The key is to seek Him first and not be content until He brings His answer.

Applying the Lessons

• *Lead by example, participate as well as preach about prayer. Support existing prayer opportunities in your congregation or establish new avenues if none exist.*

• *Seek ways to encourage collective prayer among all the churches and their leaders in your community.*

• *Encourage positive participation in the community—running for public offices, prayer walks, volunteer positions—and cover all efforts with congregational prayer.*

God Takes a Long Time

I used to think when I had a problem,
I would pray and
God would fix the problem.
I found out
God is more interested in fixing me,
and that takes a long time.

So I wait and pray
and get angry
and shake my fist at heaven
and repent and wait,
because God takes a long time.

I thought if I could memorize Scriptures,
learn formulas and find the keys,
it wouldn't take so long.
So I did.
It still took a long time.

I finally learned God isn't in a hurry.
He is watching me, waiting
to see how long
I'm going to have to wait.
My attitude influences His decision.

So I wait and pray
and praise and sing,
and smile up at heaven
(with gritted teeth)
and wait.
But it still takes a *very* long time.

8 Entering the Harvest Fields

You did not choose me, but I chose you and appointed you to go and bear fruit—fruit that will last.

JOHN 15:16

When we as a church became a praying people we certainly had no idea where God was going to take us. However, God knew and He wanted us to be prepared. Maybe it was the prayer that made us realize that somehow we were not complete. Like the prelude to my salvation experience, we began to wonder: *Is this all there is? There has to be something more.* Something was missing, but we were at a loss to know what it was. Fortunately, God was arranging our next move to show us what the "more" really was.

In 1981, we were introduced to a man by the name of Dave Cook. Dave was an ex-drug addict, ex-alcoholic, and ex-mental patient who was a musician by profession. Someone told him about our Wednesday night meeting and he came. After the meeting he approached John.

"This is what I have been looking for my whole life," he stated.

In spite of John's stares Dave continued his narrative.

"I have been in many detox programs, AA (Alcoholics Anonymous), NA (Narcotics Anonymous), and CA (Cocaine Anonymous). I've been in the mental wards of several hospitals, on bi-polar medication, and through counseling. None of that has helped me. But tonight I found the answer: It's Jesus!"

Dave was a very commanding person. He spoke rapidly and with a loud voice. Every one of his sentences was declarative and spoken about six inches from John's face. So it's not surprising that John was somewhat put off by Dave. But the man who had invited him to our church assured John that he was genuine. After many years of seeking help for his numerous addictions and resulting mental problems, that night Dave truly met the Savior.

He became a one-man gang determined to win every drug addict in the area to Jesus Christ. He began visiting the state drug abuse center, called Brandon House, where he had been a resident, and witnessed to anyone who would listen.

Dave decided he was too new to Christianity to help people grow, so he asked the director of the state drug facility if our church could come out and hold Bible studies for the residents. He could hardly wait to tell us that the director had given his consent. All this happened without our prior knowledge, so you can imagine our surprise, even dismay, when he told us *it was all arranged*.

WHY US, LORD?

God was probably laughing, seeing how stunned John and I were by this news. After all, what did we, white suburban middle-class straights, have to offer these hard-core inner-city drug addicts who were predominantly African-Americans? We had never done drugs and thought we couldn't possibly relate to addicts, but it was all set up so we had to go at least once. We actually went to the drug facility more to get Dave off our case than to answer God's call.

The plan was that I would go on Monday afternoons and meet with the women residents and John would go on Wednesday after-noons and meet with the men. So in the fall of 1981, I drove the forty-five minutes to Brandon House, almost paralyzed with fear. I took three other women with me, and we prayed in desperation most of the way. It was a good thing we had intercessory groups in place at that time because I called every one of them the day before asking them to *bombard heaven with prayer* for us. No wonder God exhorted us as a church to pray—He knew the plans He had for us would require lots of it!

I had no idea what I would say to these women. I remember sending frantic prayers up to God asking for His wisdom, all the while quoting from the first chapter of James, one of the few chapters of the Bible I had memorized. In verse 6, James says that if we doubt we won't receive the wisdom we ask for, and I was having a hard time overcoming my doubts.

To make matters worse, when we arrived at the facility the director decided he would require all twenty-five women residents to attend our first meeting. Then they could decide if they wanted to stay and continue with the Bible study.

Oh no, I thought, *now I'm going to have a bunch of angry women staring at me, daring me to say something interesting.*

My friends and I decided to tell the story behind each of our salvation experiences. None of us had very "exciting" testimonies. We were suburban housewives who had been discontented with our lives, but we hadn't done drugs, prostituted to support our habit, had our children taken away and put in foster homes, or been homeless on the streets of Chicago. I couldn't imagine our dull narratives having any effect on these streetwise women.

One by one we shared the account of our search for wholeness and the change that Jesus had made in our lives. The women just sat there, showing no emotion or change in their facial expressions while we talked. This took about forty minutes and then we released the women to leave, or remain for a short Bible study and prayer. To our astonishment every one of the women stayed.

That day God opened a door for us to Brandon House. And twenty-four years later the door is still open. "See, I have placed before you an open door that no one can shut. I know that you have little strength, yet you have kept my word and have not denied my name" (Revelation 3:8).

It was true that we had "little strength." We were forced to rely on the Holy Spirit of God. I remember the day He showed me not to look on the women's seemingly hard exteriors but to see the wounded hearts crying out to Him. In time I learned that beneath the surface we all have the same dreams and desires.

After the first Bible study, I prayed with a woman named Mary. She had earned her living as a prostitute for fifteen years, and her appearance showed the traumatic effects. She told me she felt she could not be saved because she had had several abortions. She knew what she had done was murder and didn't think God could forgive such a serious offense.

I was stunned to realize that this woman, so hardened by her way of life, knew she was violating God's law and her own conscience. This was during the time when "educated" college women were picketing in favor of abortion. I remembered Jesus' declaration to the chief priests and elders of the people: "I tell you the truth, the tax collectors and the prostitutes are entering the kingdom of God ahead of you" (Matthew 21:31).

Mary went on to successfully complete the six-month program at Brandon House. She ended up working at the same courthouse in Evanston where she had previously been arraigned and sentenced many times. We lost touch with Mary after a while, but several years later someone brought us a newspaper clipping featuring her as the first person to successfully complete an adult education course for former addicts.

Eventually the director of Brandon House decided that the afternoon meetings were taking people away from their job functions so we switched to one meeting on Monday nights with both the men and women. John worked every Monday evening, so I took over the leadership for the Bible study with two teams of people who would accompany me on alternate nights.

Although John couldn't do his Bible study with the men, he was asked to be on the board of directors of the parent organization, SASI (Substance Abuse Services, Inc.). This is a state-funded drug program with a five-million-dollar-a-year budget. Within a few years John became chairman of the board and served in that capacity for fifteen years.

Facing a Crisis Point

The beginning of a new work is exciting. Initially you are carried along by enthusiasm and hope. But working with drug addicts typically brings more failure than success. We would work diligently with someone for the six-month period of his or her stay at Brandon House. We would interact with them at the Monday evening Bible study, bus them in to our church for our Wednesday evening service, and even provide a home for them to stay in with a church member when they came out on a weekend pass. But often when they left the program they would relapse back into their old lifestyle. Some of those we had worked with even overdosed and died.

After several years I came to a crisis point. I didn't know if I wanted to continue in this work because the emotional investment was so high. I took a month off and a friend did my Bible study. During this time off I asked God to speak to me about whether or not I should continue at Brandon House.

One day I was taken by a passage in Matthew 25, where Jesus is talking about the judgment of the nations.

> Then the King will say to those on his right, "Come, you who are blessed by my Father; take your inheritance, the kingdom prepared for you since the creation of the world. For I was hungry and you gave me something to eat, I was thirsty and you gave me something to drink, I was a stranger and you invited me in, I needed clothes and you clothed me, I was sick and you looked after me, *I was in prison and you came to visit me*" (Matthew 25:34–36).

These people are in a kind of prison, I realized. *All God requires of me is that I visit them. He doesn't say anything about the results.* In that moment a burden was lifted from me. I apprehended something in my spirit that I already knew in my mind. I could go and bring them the Good News, but the results were up to God, not me.

When asked how she felt when the people she ministered to died, Mother Teresa said, "God has not called us to be successful. He has called us to be faithful."[1] Now I knew what she meant and it gave me a freedom to do God's work joyfully and faithfully without worrying about the choices the addicts would make. All I needed to be concerned about was being faithful to my calling.

Twenty-four years later I still go to Brandon House every Monday night with the message of hope and salvation. I never know who will hear and respond to the message. Often those that I thought were on fire for the Lord soon died out, while the one I hardly noticed stayed and became a member of our church. We have been able to pray with about ten-thousand addicts over the years to commit their life to Christ. We do not know the sincerity of their heart, but eternity will reveal it.

Every so often we hear from a former resident who tells us that they have gone into ministry or that they are married and raising their family in the church. Their stories are such an encouragement to "keep on keeping on." Some of them have become an integral part of our church. I would like to mention three of these wonderful people.

TROPHIES OF GRACE

Jackie

When Jackie first walked into my Bible study in the fall of 1988, she was not seeking a deeper spiritual walk but a Puerto Rican man named Pablo. Pablo was a committed member of our Bible study group, and Jackie would flirt with him during the study. Actually, they married soon after their discharge from Brandon House—but Jackie also received the Lord.

It was obvious that Jackie had been a heroin addict for twenty-two years. Her light brown skin was covered with numerous sores from dirty needles that had caused infection. She wore turtlenecks summer and winter to cover a very large mark on her neck where in desperation to find a working vein she had injected heroin.

She didn't start using drugs until after her marriage to a musician in 1967. One day she found him in the bathroom injecting himself. She had no idea he was a junkie and immediately gave him an ultimatum: "Either stop using drugs or I'm leaving you."

He told her he *couldn't stop* using drugs, it was impossible. Jackie is a very strong-willed person and couldn't imagine anyone being unable to stop such a destructive habit. *That's ridiculous!*

Anyone can stop, she reasoned. At that moment Jackie conceived a plan to prove to her husband he could stop using drugs. Without his knowledge, she had his friends inject her with heroin over the course of a month, figuring she would stop cold and show him it was possible to quit.

Sadly, by the end of the month Jackie was also a prisoner. For many years she was a functioning addict—able to work and support herself. But as her habit grew, her salary couldn't cover all the expenses so she began stealing expensive items and selling them at flea markets. She specialized in costly tools from hardware stores because of their great resale value.

Finally her lifestyle got her fired from her job and she became associated with a sophisticated check-cashing ring. They would buy stolen checks from other addicts, then change the amounts and cash the checks.

During her career in crime Jackie was arrested forty times and served sentences in three different penal institutions. Once during an argument a man put a gun to her head and pulled the trigger twice. Both times the gun jammed and her life was spared, but she never considered how miraculous this was or that she should quit her dangerous lifestyle.

Over the years she tried to rid herself of heroin. She went to every drug program in the city, but as soon as she walked out of the facility she was looking to hook up with a pusher. Finally the staff of a drug rehab program told her, "There's no help for you. We are keeping our spaces for people who really want to change." The words she had spoken to her husband twenty-two years before came back to haunt her: *If you really want to change, you can!*

The final straw came when she was arrested on a federal charge for check fraud. This time they gave her an ultimatum: "Go back to jail for a long time or go to a drug treatment center." So she ended up at Brandon House, where the Lord delivered her from her undeliverable habit.

Jackie is amazing! When she committed her life to God she never looked back. There was never the slightest shadow of desire for the drug that was her lover for twenty-two years. Even when she found Pablo, her husband of seven years, hanging from a rafter in their garage, the Lord was her refuge and strength.

Today Jackie is an indispensable staff member at Restoration Ministries (discussed further in the next chapter), where she serves as program director. She oversees many of our programs and is also in charge of the local Salvation Army Financial Assistance Program. In the fourteen years she has served the poor through our ministry she has won numerous awards, including the JCPenney Golden Rule Award.

This woman that the world dubbed incorrigible—with a rap sheet twenty pages long—became a trophy of the love of God. Everywhere she travels she shares her testimony, because she knows she has been saved only by the grace of God.

———

Ray

Ray was born at home in 1959, the same year Bibles were taken out of public schools. He was the youngest of seven children in a family with four biological fathers. Ray is a dark-skinned African-American, while several of his siblings are light-skinned. He hated facing frequent questions about the lack of family resemblance among them.

He only saw his own father three times in his life, and the last time was a frightening experience. His alcoholic father stopped by to see him and in his drunken stupor tried to kidnap him. Ray fought him, managed to jump out of his arms, and escape through a window his brother opened for him.

Perhaps that is why the gangs appealed so strongly to Ray when he moved into the projects in the sixth grade. The gang provided a family structure united by secrets, signs, and shared enemies. He wouldn't have to fend off embarrassing questions about this family there; they swore to stand by him and defend him.

By the time he was a junior in high school Ray was addicted to heroin and cocaine. He was selling drugs even under the watchful eye of the teachers in school. He wore a large snap-brim hat called the "big apple." He would make the brim stand up with newspapers, but hidden inside were bags of marijuana. When teachers made him take his hat off, all they saw were the newspapers.

Eventually he dropped out of high school and began free-basing, a method of cooking cocaine down to its purest form and smoking it. Once you start down this road of crack cocaine, you can never get enough. You will sell everything you own—clothes, cars, your own body, even your children to obtain those precious "rocks," Satan's imitation of the "pearl of great price." But this rock steals your soul and demands more and more.

In 1980, the startling news that he had a daughter stirred a desire in Ray to get clean. He tried a number of twenty-eight-day rehabs. But within a week of leaving, he would be back on drugs. During this time he married the mother of his daughter and they had three more children. He was a hustler who earned money in many different ways, including selling drugs.

Finally, in 1988, he landed back at Brandon House for the second time. He recalls hearing me share Psalm 37 with the man next to him, which happened to be the very same psalm I had shared with him the first time he went through the program. He realized God was calling him through this passage, especially verses 5–6: "Commit your way to the Lord; trust in him and he will do this: He will make your righteousness shine like the dawn, the justice of your cause like the noonday sun" (Psalm 37:5–6).

So he committed his way to the Lord. After his stay at Brandon House was completed, he entered the fledgling Harvey House, our new men's facility for men with addictive backgrounds. His wife had divorced him by this time, and he didn't have a place to live. He came thinking he would stay thirty days and left *nine years* later. He only left because he married a beautiful woman, Angela, who also came through Brandon House.

During the time of his stay at Harvey House, Ray rose through the ranks and eventually became the executive director of Restoration Ministries, a position he still holds. By a miracle of grace, his ex-wife released their four children to his care, and God provided a wonderful five-bedroom home for his family.

Ray is a recognized spiritual leader by politicians and pastors in both Harvey and South Holland. He is the chaplain for a local high school football team. *Urban Family* magazine chose Ray as one of their top-twenty-five urban role models for 1994. It's gratifying to see this man who was once a drug pusher in the projects now recognized as a role model for young men.

Lou

Another surprise God had for me at Brandon House was Lou Fonseca. When I met Lou in 1985, he was just another resident trying to deal with his addiction. Lou began his drug career in eighth grade with marijuana. Marijuana is often called the gateway drug because it opens a person up to other addictions. By his sophomore year in high school he was introduced to heroin by some older kids. That drug would be his master for the next twenty-two years.

When Lou left Brandon House after his six-month treatment he went right back to drugs. The next time I saw him was in 1994. Like many of the clients there, Lou didn't come in to stop taking drugs, he just wanted to take a break from the streets and be able to get a better high when he went back out "clean."

So Lou left again and went right back to his heroin. Lou's brother Craig was also addicted and had been to Brandon House twice. But he decided he had had enough and was admitted to our eighteen-month program at Harvey House. Craig asked the men there to pray for his brother. He often told Lou that he needed to go into the program also.

By 1997, Lou was doing speedballs—a dangerous mixture of heroin and cocaine. One night as Lou and a friend were driving to pick up their cocaine for the speedballs, Lou couldn't resist taking a hit of heroin. He overdosed and slumped over in the car. His friend immediately got off the expressway, pulled up to Cook County Hospital's emergency room, and left him there.

Fortunately, the doctor was able to revive Lou, and as he was signing his release papers he mentioned, "You must have a guardian angel watching over you."

"Why's that?" asked Lou.

"Because if you had been dropped off *one minute later* you would have been dead!"

Finally God had Lou's attention, and two weeks later he entered our drug rehab program. By the grace of God and the prayers of His people, Lou was able to kick his twenty-two-year heroin addiction by quitting "cold turkey."

During his years as an addict Lou was arrested thirty-one times and had twenty-nine convictions. He also served two prison terms and was sure he would die an addict. But God had other plans. Not only has Lou been free from drugs for eight years, but for the last six years he has been my son-in-law, living with our daughter Shannon right next door! I often mention to Shannon, little did I know when I went out to Brandon House in 1981 that I was going to find her a husband. Our God is full of wonderful surprises, and Lou has certainly been one of the best.

The Treasures of Darkness

Thirty years ago, while reading Isaiah, I was captured by a particular verse: "I will give you the treasures of darkness, riches stored in secret places, so that you may know that I am the Lord, the God of Israel, who summons you by name" (Isaiah 45:3).

It wasn't until about ten years later, when I was deeply involved in our ministry with drug addicts, that I realized Brandon House was the treasure house where God's riches were stored. Who would have known that many of God's choice jewels, like Ray, Jackie, and Lou would be found in such a place?

I am always amazed by the beauty in the souls of some of these men and women who have suffered so greatly in life. As a pearl forms because of an irritating speck deep inside an oyster, these people have been forged through suffering—in the dreadful projects, through neglect, abuse, incest, abandonment, or a substance that has destroyed their life. But when God calls them out of their "secret places," what often emerges is a radiant faith, its brilliance unmistakable.

The successes I have shared from our time at Brandon House, though, should be kept in perspective. We had many more instances of discouragement and trials of faith during those early years. In one example, one of the men we ministered to robbed the house of the church treasurer because he thought he would find money there.

Still, God was at work in our midst, protecting us in our ignorance of addictive behaviors. No one suffered any harm or grave loss during all those years. This fact is amazing, considering that a number of people in the church invited the addicts into their homes on the weekends when they were given a pass to leave the state-run center.

After working with the clients at the state drug program for a year, we realized that we were losing too many of our new converts to the streets when they went back home to the same people, places, and things that were a part of their addictive lifestyle.

So we began to pray for a building where they could live and be trained in the ways of God before they were released into the world. But it was a challenging problem to solve. Where would we find a building, get the necessary financial help, and the right person to run the program? It all sounded overwhelming but, as usual, God had already prepared the *next step* of our journey for us.

Applying the Lessons

- *Great ministry opportunities are sometimes "dropped" on us from unlikely sources. If you have disregarded something because it came out of nowhere, reconsider it in the light of Scripture. Pray with key people of faith in your church to determine if it is something put in motion by God himself.*

- *Look around your congregation and see if there are any "pearls"— people whose faith has been forged out of great difficulty and suffering in life. If so, think about how they can be used of God to encourage other people from similar backgrounds.*

- *Seek the Lord to discover the next step in your church's destiny.*

Opal

You taught me
to see more clearly today
as you sat and
shared your life.

Your words became a finger
to wipe away the steam
on my darkly glass,
a peephole
into imperishable treasure.

Tears flowed,
for no one gazing into eternal truth
can remain unmoved.
You sat, head bowed,
simple speech, revealing
the beauty of the unexpected.

Aptly are you named
Opal;
not the glittering fire
of a ruby,
nor the deep, exotic stirrings
of an emerald,
but the grace of transparency,
revealing inner treasure.

Thank you,
for that glimpse of divinity
within your earthen vessel.

The Next Step

*In his heart a man plans his course, but
the Lord determines his steps.*

PROVERBS 16:9

When God opened the door to the state drug center, we
had to step out in faith. It was like Alice stepping through the
looking glass into a new world of strange and unfamiliar creatures.
Some were frightening, and certainly the planet of the poor and
disadvantaged holds real danger for the unenlightened and neo-
phyte sojourner. But we were blissfully unaware of that. In our
enthusiasm, optimism, and ignorance we thought we knew exactly
what to do next.

As I mentioned previously, when God gives us a vision, we
usually set about to bring it into fulfillment in our own strength.
This instance was a good example of that tendency. The male
addicts needed a place to stay when they left Brandon House, so
we immediately launched out to meet that need. In late 1982, we
rented a home and confidently named it Nicodemus House.

This venture did not go as planned. In fact, Nicodemus House
was a disaster! One of the men spent his time out in the backyard
getting high sniffing from a gasoline can, the house was set on fire
when one of the men fell asleep smoking, and two of our donated

cars disappeared with the men who took them.

We weren't discouraged, though. The flesh is strong-willed and we were not ready to give up yet. We rented another house, which also fell apart. Most of the men went back to their old habits and neighborhoods.

Finally, in 1984, we *gave up our dream* of having a Christian home—a place for recovering addicts to study the Bible, find healing for the deep issues in their lives, learn job skills, and be restored to their families and communities. We had hoped that these men would return to the streets with the good news to set other captives free. But since nothing we tried worked out, we finally gave up.

THE DREAM IS RESURRECTED

For several years we stopped thinking about a home for addicts and ministered to those who wanted to stay connected to our church. We helped some of them find housing and jobs nearby, and a small number became part of our church.

Then, in 1987, something happened that caused us to hope again in the dream. We reconnected with Manny Gonzales, a Mexican-American man who had been a client at Brandon House in 1984. We saw him at a Christian conference and found out that he was still on fire for God. He also shared the same vision we had had for a men's home.

Manny was a forty-six-year-old man who landed in the state drug facility (Brandon House) under a program called TASC (Treatment Alternative to Street Crime). It was either deal with his drug problem or go to jail again. He had been on drugs since the age of twelve and had risen quickly in the pecking order of the drug world, becoming a leader in drug sales in his area. How he was converted in that Bible study is still a mystery to me, but not to the Holy Spirit. "The wind blows wherever it pleases. You hear its sound, but you cannot tell where it comes from or where it is going. So it is with everyone born of the Spirit" (John 3:8).

John and I seemed to know intuitively: This is the man. Our previous failures were because we never had the right man for the job. The people we put in charge of our homes were single men who were committed to the Lord but had no experience with drugs. Now it seems ridiculous that we thought these men could deal with addictive behaviors. (I believe I mentioned previously that we were enthusiastic and optimistic, but ignorant.)

When we set out to find a building, we knew God wanted the home to be in Harvey, an extremely distressed southern suburb of Chicago that borders our village of South Holland. Before this time we would not have had the faith to take this step. Harvey was once the jewel of the southern suburbs, but after the steel mill and other businesses closed in the town, decay set in. It was filled with poverty, prostitution, gang bangers, drive-by shootings, fatherless homes, and neglected children—not the sort of place we would normally choose to put a home for recovering addicts.

The first building we tried to buy was the old Lion's Club building. It was a beautiful three-story home right near downtown Harvey. However, the mayor would not sell us the building, even though we offered a good price.

In retrospect, we could see that we had the right dream but the wrong location. So we continued looking until we found an old flea-bitten motel that was a haven for drug deals and prostitution. It wasn't beautiful or desirable—but it was God's choice.

Worth the Wait

In God's kingdom several things must come into play at the same time in order to see success. The right location is one of the elements, but there is also the matter of timing. When we first tried to implement this plan for a men's home, we weren't ready for the ministry. Our hearts were unprepared and too naïve for the task. Over time God trained us in knowing how to interact with addictive behaviors. The disappointments and failures were key to getting us ready for His plan. When the time was right, and when Manny was sufficiently trained to provide the leadership, we had no trouble finding the right place to begin.

The delay accomplished other good things as well. John had the time to establish a separate ministry—Restoration Ministries—that could operate independently from our church. He knew that for other churches to feel free to send their people as volunteers, we would need a separate organization. So he established a board of directors from different churches and occupations to oversee the ministry. Because it consisted of well-respected men and women in the community, the ministry enjoyed immediate acceptance and credibility from the other churches.

Once we paid the down payment on the motel, the men of the church went at the building with hammers, saws, and crowbars with all the fervor of a new dream becoming reality. As the mice and cockroaches left the building for greener pastures, intercessors attacked with spiritual warfare to rid the building of unclean spirits. Then we declared Jesus as Lord over the property. Our friend and fellow pastor Ben Essenburg declared, "The day Restoration Ministries moved into Harvey, Harvey became a better place!"

This is a very powerful and true statement. The followers of Jesus Christ should shape the world rather than the world defining the church. In the eighteen years that Restoration Ministries has been serving the poor in Harvey, Harvey *has* become a better place. Many of the abandoned buildings that served as drug dens have been torn down; the crime rate, once the highest in the suburbs, is declining; and new businesses have come into the area, which means more jobs for the unskilled labor force of the poor.

It is amazing to see that this multiracial, desperately poor suburb has become the fertile soil for our peripheral growth as a church. Although our church has not greatly increased in numbers (with people coming and going, we remain around two to three hundred adults), we have grown significantly in other ways. Essentially, we have grown out into the community where we can impact many more people than would ever attend a church service. Thirty new Christian ministries have emerged in Harvey and South Holland as we have experienced an interlacing of political and religious structures in the two villages. This is all the Lord's work, resulting from our learning how to be obedient to His call.

A CIRCLE OR A VINE?

My husband's friend Pastor Charles Simpson noted in one of his letters that while churches often succeed in growth within, they generally fail in their mission to fill the earth with the knowledge of the glory of the Lord (Habakkuk 2:14). He believes the reason is that some churches adopt a circle as their model and others pattern themselves after a vine.

> A circle is inanimate—not living. It is a single round closed line with a center. . . . A circle includes everything within it and excludes everything outside of it. . . . We see the church as something to go *to*, not from. The church circle is something we join—not each other. Church circles are often built around a particular doctrine or method, or even less worthy, a particular convenience. Often church life becomes an orbit of activity. Our time and resources are consumed by the circle. Then our personal circle becomes a matter of including or excluding based upon who is in or out of the church circle.
>
> *A worse part about a circle mentality is that it all too often ends where it begins. That is, even after all of our best efforts at preaching, teaching, and worshipping, we only maintain what we started.*[1]

This very accurately describes the condition of some sectors of the church today. Most of the finances, staff, volunteers, and energy go into maintaining the status quo of the church—not in fulfilling the Great Commission. Numbers, buildings, and programs within the circle measure church success in our postmodern society rather than how well we are impacting the world around us.

Charles Simpson continues to describe the true purpose of the church: It is to be a vine.

> While the circle is inanimate, the vine is a living plant. The circle is a closed figure, but the vine is an outward moving one. . . . The vine church is rooted in eternal life and eternal truth. . . . Jesus himself is that root and vine-trunk. . . . The vine church is extended by branches that are truly joined to one another (see Ephesians 4:16).
>
> The vine church is not highly centralized; it is not personality or program driven. It is driven by the life and character of Jesus (His DNA). The vine church covers the ground, goes through, over, and around, as each new branch reaches out. It

is opportunistic, clasping onto what lies before it.

The vine church not only relates to its life and itself, it relates to the world before it—business, labor, and professions—wherever it finds itself. It is not programmed from without, but from the life within. It is never confounded by obstacles; it climbs them and goes on. *It does not say, "Come to us," it says, "We are coming to you."*[2]

Jesus said His church would be "sent out" ones to go into the entire world. So why do we wait for the world to come to us? Often when we think of "all the world," we associate it with mission trips to foreign countries. Of course this meaning is included, but that interpretation is too narrow. Just before Jesus was taken up into heaven after the resurrection, He gave these instructions to his followers:

> But you will receive power when the Holy Spirit comes on you; and you will be my witnesses in Jerusalem, and in all Judea and Samaria, and to the ends of the earth. (Acts 1:8)

Their witness of the risen Christ would begin in their hometown of Jerusalem and then spread out to the "ends of the earth." If we are not a witness where we live, we have nothing to export. If we can't impact the community we live in, how do we expect to impact a third-world country?

Jesus didn't just stand in the temple teaching and expect the people to come to Him. He walked among them. "As he went along, he saw a man blind from birth" (John 9:1). This encounter became a teaching lesson for the disciples, a healing for the blind man, and a confrontation with the Pharisees. But it wouldn't have happened in the confines of the temple.

Leaving Our Comfort Zone

When we left our comfort zone to step into the intimidating world of drug addicts, God opened the way before us. Out of that original refurbished motel that came to be known as Harvey House, He has birthed many more ministries. He has given us favor with the various mayors that have held office and has raised up a substantial donor base to support all the ongoing ministries. He has made buildings available when we needed them, and for each new project, He has brought us the right person for the job.

In John 15, Jesus calls himself the true vine and says we are His branches. He warns us that we cannot bear fruit unless we remain in Him, but if we are in Him, we will bear much fruit. He also says, "You did not choose me, but I chose you and appointed you to *go* and bear fruit—fruit that will last" (John 15:16).

Many Christians believe that Jesus was speaking only about the fruit the Holy Spirit produces in our lives (love, joy, peace). But the analogy of the vine speaks of branches spreading out in all directions and producing fruit: "Go into all the world and preach the good news to all creation" (Mark 16:15). To quote Charles Simpson again: "He was talking about reproductivity—spawning new branches and bearing reproductive fruit that reached the world."[3]

Just as a plant that is left to remain in the pot becomes *root-bound,* so many Christians in the circle church model become *program bound.* Their lives revolve around the church and its programs, but they never leave the confines of that circle. A root-bound plant will ultimately die because the pot is only meant to hold and nourish the plant in its early development. The knowledgeable gardener will transplant it to a place where it can truly grow and spread out.

Each of us in the body of Christ is a branch from our true vine, Christ. The purpose of a vine is to grow and produce fruit. Unfortunately, many of us in the church are root-bound, and we wonder why we are so spiritually apathetic. If we do not fulfill the purpose for which we were created—to grow outwardly—we will soon become bored and restless with acquiring knowledge that never produces fruit. We will become seekers after the "American Dream" rather than seekers after God's will.

Many Christians today wander from church to church, looking for something because they are bored with the confines of the "pot." The nature of Christ within them witnesses to their spirit that there is more to life than they are living, but they aren't sure what they are looking for. So they wander.

"Nearly one-fifth of all churchgoers now attend more than one church, usually on a rotating basis, in order to meet their spiritual needs and satisfy their theological curiosity."[4] As church leaders for thirty-three years, John and I have seen this developing trend. People today hesitate to make a commitment because they are on a search for spiritual enlightenment and they want the freedom to choose a church based on their particular need at the moment.

Seemingly, we have forgotten that our Lord "did not come to be served, but to serve" (Matthew 20:28). And we are asked to do the same. "Deny yourself" is a distasteful idea to the average American churchgoer who has been convinced by wrong theology that God exists to serve us and eagerly awaits our latest request.

Voices calling in the wilderness warn that the church in America has become irrelevant, but we are not streaming out to the desert to hear the news. Rather, we dismiss those who are called fanatics in camel's hair clothing.

The church can make two errors in response to the criticism that we are no longer relevant. First, we can become like the world and conduct our churches as a profitable business with programs to keep everybody happy and busy. Or we can refuse to change and lose all hope of reaching the younger generation.

God's answer to our problem of irrelevancy is to repent of our self-centered lifestyle and respond to the overwhelming needs around us. "Open your eyes and look at the fields! They are ripe for harvest" (John 4:35).

When the Lord opened the door to Restoration Ministries, we were amazed at all the need out there—beyond the reach of the insulated church-family circle. Sometimes it can be overwhelming: "How far will they go among so many?" (John 6:9). Other times we are discouraged as we set a new ministry in place to reach the lost and can't find enough volunteers to make it happen. We know the truth of Jesus' words: "The harvest is plentiful but the workers are few" (Matthew 9:37). Many of us in our church are stretched to the breaking point, and still the people come. It often feels like we are bailing out a boat that is going to sink anyway. Like my crisis of faith concerning the drug ministry, John has also had his moment of despair.

He was driving to Brandon House for his Wednesday afternoon Bible study, accompanied by Tony Salerno, a former client of the clinic and now a functioning member of our church. John was discussing his misgivings about the ministry and the number of men who had recently relapsed.

"I don't know if all the time and money is worth the investment, Tony. Look at all the men we thought were delivered and are now back on drugs," John lamented.

"Well, would it be worth all the time and money if only one soul was saved for all eternity?" Tony asked.

"Yes," said John, "One soul would be worth it."

"Well," said Tony, "I'm that one."

That conversation was a great reminder to John. He never wondered again about the time and effort put in. He knew it was worth it. Of course, God in His goodness has saved many more than Tony. While there has been a great failure rate in the drug ministry, there have also been wonderful successes that have impacted entire families.

When you work with drug addicts and the disadvantaged, you have to throw out the numbers philosophy of the American church. It is not about numbers, but about *individuals that the Father is seeking.* When an addict is saved and delivered from drugs, often the way of life changes for the entire family. The children are especially impacted for good. Many of the women who go through our program are able to get their children back from foster homes. We try to send the men back to their homes as wage earners and spiritual leaders to their wives and children.

I believe that we are seeing the parable of the great banquet in Luke 14:16–24 being literally fulfilled. In that parable, those who were originally invited to the banquet were too busy with the cares and concerns of daily life to respond. The kingdom of God was not their first priority. But those who were just hanging out on the street corner benefited from their indifference.

The addicts and prostitutes we approach do not realize at first what they are being invited to. What a blessing it is for us to bring to them an invitation to the banquet of the ages, a banquet thrown by God himself!

How God Has Changed Me

The change I have witnessed in the addicts over the years is nothing compared to the change God has worked in my own life. I had all the false assumptions about the addicts and the poor in our midst: *Well, if they wanted a job they could get one. If they weren't so lazy, they could get out of the projects. Addicts have chosen their lifestyle, so why should I help them?*

Twenty-four years of ministry have taught me differently. Most of the people I've met are people who take drugs to deal with the overwhelming pain of their existence. I have heard stories that have shocked me and caused me to weep at the inhumanity of man. I've also been awed by the courage and forgiveness demonstrated by these people. These are some of the bravest people I have ever known, and thankfully many are open to the saving gospel of Jesus Christ.

They have also taught me about an attribute of God I had little knowledge of before—grace. Being prophetic in my gifting, I love to study and teach the Word of God. I also love rules and have a healthy fear of God, but for years I never understood grace. Never, that is, until I began taking the gospel to what some would call the "dregs" of society—the prostitutes and drug addicts. Among them, God began to show me the truth.

Before this time, my greatest desire was to be a well-known Bible teacher; I often pictured myself before an audience of thousands who were hanging on my every word. I thank God now that He did not allow that to happen. If He had, I probably would never have understood grace. An amazing thing happens when you minister to people considered the very least in society. What you give out comes back to you *multiplied*. As I spoke to them about the love of God, I realized that I was loved too, not for what I did but for who I am.

In Galatians 2, Paul went to Jerusalem to submit his fourteen-year-old ministry among the Gentiles to the church authorities for their approval. The elders at Jerusalem recognized that Paul had heard from God and was doing God's work, but their caution to him was "We should continue to remember the poor" (Galatians 2:10). Interesting! It is as if God is saying, this is the thing that validates a call from God. Or God's heart is always toward the poor, so don't forget them. Could it be that this is God's litmus test for ministry?

I don't know the answer to the above, but I do know that the disadvantaged can respond to the gospel with abandonment because they have nothing to lose. They

> **The disadvantaged can respond to the gospel with abandonment because they have nothing to lose.**

are needy and vulnerable and often remind me how self-satisfied and secure I am. Someone has said that the main reason we lose our "first love" is because we lose our sense of needing God. Every week at the Bible study I am reminded of my own neediness and refreshed by my students' trust in God.

I have often wondered why this ministry to the addicts is so appealing to me. Most of them have been reduced to the core of their being; there are no glittering images to present to others. The only way for most of them is up because they have bottomed out. The only ones we can't help are those who don't see themselves as desperate. They feel the drugs are just a temporary problem, not a revelation of who they are.

As I experience the Holy Spirit loving them through me, I realize that I am lovable also, not just the person I present to the world, but that other base person within that I have never truly conquered.

In John 13, after Jesus finished washing the disciples' feet, he began to teach them the significance of what He had done. He explained that even though He was their Lord and teacher, He was willing to humble himself to become a lowly servant. He knew that it was time "to leave this world and go to the Father." So "he now showed them the full extent of his love" (v.1). This powerful lesson on the eve of his crucifixion was clear: God's love manifests itself as servanthood. He then told His disciples, "Now that you know these things, you will be blessed if you do them" (John 13:17).

When churches begin to move out of their comfort zone, their little circle, and become like a vine, serving their communities with the power of God's love, then they can fully understand the truth of Jesus' words to His disciples. They will find blessing and happiness in unexpected ways and in unexpected places.

George Whitfield, the fiery preacher who was a contemporary of John Wesley, preached to the coal miners of England. A group of people who were illiterate, impoverished, and of a volatile temperament, they were not a preacher's choice audience. Yet he wrote in his journal, "I believe I was never more acceptable to my Master than when I was standing to teach those hearers in the open fields. Some may censure me, but if I thus please men I should not be servant of Christ."[5]

I am so thankful that Jesus has trusted our church with these "bruised reeds" and "smoldering wicks" (Matthew 12:20) of society. He has given us the grace to keep from snuffing out those wicks and instead fan the flame of His love. My life would be very different without them. I always have the sense that when I am caring for the "least of these" I am pleasing my Master. And that knowledge brings joy to my heart.

Applying the Lessons

- *Continue to pray and trust God for any dreams that have not yet been fulfilled. Remember, both timing and logistics must line up with God's will before a dream can be realized.*

- *Meet with your church staff to discuss which model your church has adopted (a circle or a vine). If necessary, set in motion plans to change it according to the pattern of John 15.*

- *Take a hard look at your current programs to see if any of them reaches out beyond your comfort zone. Pray for God's guidance in reaching out into the needy community outside the church family and building.*

The Call

God has called each one
to walk a road
in this life.

It is not the path
you would choose,
but His sovereign choice,
because your Creator
knows you better
than you know yourself.

Joy should impel you, but
your disagreement with Him
keeps you in the valley and
fuels your charge
that He was wrong.

Do you want to know joy
in the midst of turmoil, or
fulfillment during times of failure?

Accept His way,
cease your struggle, and you will know
your Father's acceptance.

Then the circumstances
will not be an enemy to be resisted
but God's mentor
to form you into the image
of His blessed Son.

The Bonds of Unity

*Make every effort to keep the unity of the
Spirit through the bond of peace. There is
one body and one Spirit.*

EPHESIANS 4:3–4

During the late '70s we became good friends with a
charismatic reformed pastor and his wife. This man took John to
the ministerial meeting once a month in South Holland. It wasn't
long before a few of the ministers began asking questions about
my husband's ordination, and it didn't take too many questions to
discover he wasn't ordained. It was politely requested that he stop
attending the meeting.

In typical John fashion, he announced this when he walked in
the door that night after work.

"Well, I got kicked out of the ministerial association this morning!"

John has never suffered from a spirit of rejection so he thought
it was quite amusing. He didn't take it personally and was glad for
the three meetings he did attend, since they taught him something
that would be of great benefit later on. His predominant memory
from the meetings he attended was a Baptist pastor and a Christian Reformed pastor who mostly argued doctrine. He saw no
decisions made by the members that would impact their village.

By the late '80s the ministerial association was just about defunct. Most of the ministers in town were John's patients and many had become good friends over the years. They respected his wisdom, and by then our church was no longer considered a "cult." We had proved to be sound in our doctrine and our support of the village. So John was invited to become part of the ministerial association again, and a few months later he was elected president—even though he still wasn't formally ordained.

From his past experience, John realized the meeting format had to change in order to survive. The competitive spirit that existed between the ministers didn't foster friendship or unity. John changed the meeting to a luncheon that was hosted by our church in the beginning. This time slot drew more men, and the free lunch had its own appeal.

Immediately the atmosphere was different. The ministers were more relaxed sitting around a table and interacting. The prevailing attitude changed from competition to friendship. They began to see they were all in the same boat working for the same goal—the kingdom of God. Many friendships were forged during those times of laughter and conversation; as a result, they were able to plan events that would bring that same unity to the village. John knew from Scripture that unity had to come first to the local leaders in the body of Christ before it could reach other parts of the community.

During these ministerial meetings the representative churches were often asked to donate to the various church-sponsored village events. The other ministers were always intrigued that John was able to pledge money without getting approval from a consistory board. So many of the pastors couldn't make any decision without running it past the ruling body of their church. John's answer was astonishing to them: "My deacons and elders trust my decision."

Bob, one of the young, dynamic pastors in the group, began to balk at the restraints of his consistory board on his vision for the church. In time he disbanded the board and then asked John if Brian Kamstra, our worship leader, could teach them how to worship. At that time their worship consisted of singing a few hymns from the Psalter, and Bob wanted to introduce contemporary songs into their service.

Brian went every Saturday morning for a year to meet with Bob's musicians. The first couple of months they just stood around the piano while Brian played and taught them how to enter into genuine worship. Of course, when that happens God responds—and it wasn't long before people were receiving healing and becoming bonded together in unity. Then it was time to bring the new worship experience to the congregation on Sunday morning.

After a few months of this new contemporary worship, some of the older conservative people left the church. But this church soon became the fastest-growing congregation in our village for the young, reformed churchgoing crowd. As a result, several other churches asked Brian to come and teach them how to worship too.

Every November we had a special night of music the Wednesday before Thanksgiving. Brian invited Bob's church to join us after that first year of working with their choir, and it was an amazing success. This has become a tradition with us; we usually have about six churches participating in the event.

It's wonderful when the body of Christ gathers to praise and worship our Lord in a spirit of unity without competition or rancor. We have found supernatural favor on these nights in fulfillment of the Word of God.

> How good and pleasant it is when brothers live together in unity! It is like precious oil poured on the head, running down on the beard, running down on Aaron's beard, down upon the collar of his robes. It is as if the dew of Hermon were falling on Mount Zion. For *there the Lord bestows his blessing,* even life forevermore. (Psalm 133)

It is interesting to see people come into the concert tentatively, with closed faces, and then see them by the end of the worship time hugging, crying, and introducing themselves to others as the oil of the Holy Spirit flows in response to exalting the Lord Jesus Christ. No wonder the devil fights us so much in this area of unity!

THE REST OF THE TOWN IS BROUGHT IN

We have a wonderful, Spirit-filled Christian mayor, Don De Graff, who always attends our Thanksgiving worship service. One night after the concert he asked Brian if we could do the same type of thing for the entire town. Out of that discussion we decided to produce "God With Us," a choral program from Integrity Music.

Brian directed the worship band, and Ed Lindquist, a worship leader from another church, directed the two-hundred-fifty-voice choir. We presented "God With Us" in May 1996 in the field house of our local high school. Sixteen churches were represented in the choir and band, and the field house was packed with people representing every major Christian denomination in South Holland.

The program was such a success that we repeated it in 1997. Then in 1999, we produced "God for Us," and in 2002, "God in Us." In 2001 and 2003, we presented the Brooklyn Tabernacle Choir's program called "High and Lifted Up." This musical incorporates the multiracial dimension of our village with patriotic songs and mainstream choral numbers.

It is impossible to put into words the impact of many churches working together to exalt the Lord Jesus. We saw differences put aside, friendships created, the kingdom of God becoming reality, and life reflecting a little taste of heaven.

After the success of our first "God With Us," the pastors decided to hold ongoing village praise gatherings in the park on the Fourth of July and Labor Day weekends. People from the village churches gather in the park on a Sunday evening to sing praise songs and hear a speaker. Together we proclaim that Jesus Christ is the Lord over our town.

Jesus said that our unity as believers is what would convince the world of God's reality. We know that the early church had great power. "Everyone was filled with awe, and many wonders and miraculous signs were done by the apostles" because "*all the believers were together* and had everything in common" (Acts 2:43–44).

Faithfulness to Our Call Is What Counts

Now two thousand years later, we have a hard time creating unity within our own church congregations, and to find unity with others in the wider body of Christ is even harder. The problem? We are rife with envy, jealousy, backbiting, and criticism. More often than not pastors' meetings become competitive functions with the "numbers game" being played. But if the number of our followers determines our success, then at His death Jesus was a total failure.

When my husband, John, allowed our worship leader to help Bob's church, the result was that they became the fastest-growing church in town. A few of our people even left to go there. They far surpassed the number of people in our congregation, and we could have been discouraged if we didn't have a kingdom vision: It's not about us but about extending God's kingdom.

Our success is not measured by the size of our congregation but by our faithfulness to the plan of God for us. Each church has a special function in the body, and we have to be careful not to try to emulate another church with a different calling. We must be true to our calling even if it seems small and insignificant.

Moses was called by God to build a tabernacle where God could dwell in the midst of His people. "Then have them make a sanctuary for me, and I will dwell among them. Make this tabernacle and all its furnishings exactly like the pattern I will show you" (Exodus 25:8–9).

In Numbers 1–4, we see that God assigned each of the twelve tribes a *specific place to camp around the tabernacle,* the place where God would dwell in their midst. God wanted their lives to be centered on Him in all things. He made it clear to Moses that there was to be no deviation from His plan.

God is a God of order, evident by His meticulous care in setting up the camp around the tabernacle. All the tribes were assigned the spot where they were to dwell on each of the four compass points—three on the east, three on the south, three on the west, and three on the north. Moses, Aaron, and Aaron's sons also dwelt on the east at the door of the tabernacle. Each division of three tribes had their own banner or standard displayed in the camp. The most well-known was the banner of Judah, which depicted a lion.

When the pillar of cloud moved, they had to tear down the camp and follow God. Every tribe in the camp had a specific task to do and each had a special place to march in the procession. The tribe of Judah, which means "praise of Jehovah," led the way with several other tribes and wagons carrying the curtains, coverings, hangings, gate, and door of the tabernacle. Other tribes were responsible for dismantling the various parts of the structure and loading the items onto wagons.

The Kohathites, from the priestly tribe of Levi, were responsible for carrying the ark of the covenant in the middle of the procession because *God had to be in the midst*. The last tribe in the procession was Naphtali. These specific places and job assignments for the tribes were not subject to change.

I believe the same concept holds true for the church today. God has given each church a place to dwell on this earth where they will bring Him the most glory: "He determined the times set for them and the exact places where they should live" (Acts 17:26).

The tribe of Naphtali couldn't complain that they were the last in line because that was God's place for them. If we could choose the place for our church, I'm sure it would be in some beautiful town high in the mountains of Colorado. But God placed us, Spirit of God Fellowship, in South Holland, Illinois. This is the only place where we can fulfill our destiny.

Each tribe also had a specific function to carry out. The others could have murmured against the Kohathites, because they had the privilege of carrying the ark of the covenant, which symbolized the presence of God. To other tribes the role given to the Kohathites may have seemed more important than all the rest, but God didn't see it that way. Even the tribe who pulled out the pegs holding the fence in place around the tabernacle was indispensable.

In the New Testament, God compares us to a body, with each part fulfilling a special function. Although the passage in 1 Corinthians 12 is talking about individual members, it could just as well be applied to individual churches that make up His body. Paul makes the case for each of us fulfilling our role and not complaining about what that role is or envying another's function.

> But in fact God has arranged the parts in the body, every one of them, *just as he wanted them to be*. If they were all one part, where would the body be? As it is, there are many parts, but one body. . . .
>
> But God has combined the members of the body and has given greater honor to the parts that lacked it, so that there should be no division in the body, but that its parts should have equal concern for each other. (1 Corinthians 12:18–20; 24–25)

When all the Hebrew tribes were in their correct position in the camp, the view from the mountain revealed the arrangement of the tents was in the shape of a cross. The dark tents made of badger skin spread out as the four arms of the cross, and the tabernacle where God dwelt was in the very center. In a similar way, when each church is in its assigned position, doing what God has given us to do, we represent the cross to the world.

Up to this point the world has seen the body of Christ as disjointed parts, competing with each other and envying those who seem to have the more important job. We don't want to march at the end of the procession; we want to be first in line. We want to be bearers of the ark, not pullers of the pegs.

We attend seminars that give us the seven or ten or twelve essential steps to build our church . . . and "building the church" always implies increasing the number of members. We go home and implement man's wisdom, and even though we may have initial success, there will be no remaining fruit. Jesus told Peter, "I will build my church" (Matthew 16:18). He still means it!

THE THREE W'S

In the tabernacle of Moses there were three types of people: worshipers, workers, and warriors. Each man knew his job and did it. In the same way, each individual church has been called primarily to a specific job function, although we must not neglect the other functions. Some churches are famous for their worship, and they will help the rest of us in the body to learn how to worship better. Others are superb warriors or intercessors, and I have personally learned much from these dedicated soldiers. Some, like Mike Bickle's church in Kansas City, have combined worship and intercession as battle strategy that they employ twenty-four hours a day.

These intercessors are the "air power" of the spiritual battle. Modern air power softens up the more difficult targets for the ground forces that will follow. Since men first began fighting battles, war was about taking territory from the enemy—and that remains true today. However, air power is not enough to win the war. It is still the infantrymen on the ground—the "ground force"—who put themselves at great risk by marching into hostile territory to defeat the enemy hand-to-hand. This is the only sure way to win back ground lost to the enemy.

Our church, Spirit of God Fellowship, has been called to be part of God's ground force. Part of the third W (workers), we are the ones who engage in the hand-to-hand combat; we see the faces and realize the humanness of the battle. If we didn't move in and take the ground that the intercessors have prepared, the battle could not be won. It is often dirty, discouraging work, and the greatest casualties are always in the ground force.

It doesn't sound like a very desirable vocation, but service to the poor and disadvantaged is an extremely rewarding life. Of course, we have learned to worship and how to battle by intercession through the contribution of others in the body, but our *primary calling* is that of a worker. Sometimes it involves hard physical work, and other times it is simply giving hope to the drug addict who believes God has passed him by. When we embrace our unique calling it becomes our passion.

Whatever our particular area of competency might be, God has also called each of us to strive for unity in the body of Christ. Without that unity all of our efforts to proclaim Him Lord will fall short, because God has ordained that it is *through our unity* that the world will believe. If we are to reflect God to this world, we must reflect the unity present in the Godhead. I'm not talking about a unity brought about by compromise. I mean an organic unity that is possible with all brothers and sisters who declare Jesus as Lord and are fully committed to His Word.

Frontline Soldiers Take the Hits

I mentioned Patrice Kamstra in chapter 7. She heads up the group of intercessors from various churches in our town called Hands Across the Village. Of all the things the devil hates, I think he most hates intercessors who pray for unity—and Patrice was the catalyst of this intercession.

Three years ago she was diagnosed with cancer and has been through surgery, chemotherapy, and radiation. Yet through it all she kept her commitment to the prayer group. Today she is healed and walking in the joy and fullness of Christ. It is the frontline soldiers who take the most hits, and she is definitely in the front lines of a furious battle.

In the past I fit the old adage "Fools rush in where angels fear to tread" by my impulsive decisions. I was one of those soldiers who runs into the battle with a great deal of enthusiasm but forgets her armor and weapons. Fortunately, age and battle scars have made me a little wiser.

I still love the battle, but I have learned to seek God in prayer and to follow Paul's excellent advice: "Put on the full armor of God so that you can take your stand against the devil's schemes" (Ephesians 6:11). Every Christian is called to be a soldier of Christ Jesus, but many prefer to spend their time "involved in civilian affairs" (2 Timothy 2:4).

Every Christian is called to "make every effort to keep the unity of the Spirit through the bond of peace" (Ephesians 4:3). But when we engage in intercession as one means of achieving this unity, we need to be aware of the devil's schemes. Many don't understand the fury of the devil against the people of God who dare to strive for unity, but we do!

Three years ago we started interceding in earnest for God's glory to be revealed in our church and in our town. As I mentioned in another chapter, our house churches alternate fasting and praying throughout the work week. During this time many families in the church have experienced illness or some other trial of faith. We came to realize that if the devil was attacking us so passionately, then we must be doing something right. This has given us the impetus to keep going.

We have also seen that God is using these testing situations to produce perseverance in us and to reveal areas of our life that need to be brought in line with the Word of God. I think all of us who have suffered a trial of faith would gladly go through it again, because *we are not defeated by these experiences.* "No, in all these things we are more than conquerors through him who loved us" (Romans 8:37). With that knowledge we can fight on, no matter what comes against us.

UNITY: THE HEART CRY OF JESUS

There is no formula for bringing about unity, but we do know that it must begin first in our hearts and then be demonstrated in our lives by the Holy Spirit. Brian, our worship leader, has found that unity is not about a shared function or a crusade. That type of coming together produces a great one-night event, but it does not necessarily foster ongoing relationships.

"Unity," to quote Brian, "happens around a coffee table as friendships are birthed and we learn to love and appreciate one another." The heart cry of our Savior in His high priestly prayer just before His death was that all of His disciples would come into the same unity that He experienced with the Father.

> I have given them the glory that you gave me, that they may be one as we are one: I in them and you in me. May they be brought to complete unity to let the world know that you sent me and have loved them even as you have loved me. (John 17:22–23)

Jesus' purpose in giving us His glory is first of all to display the unity present in the Godhead. This is not a unity brought about by conformity, discussion, or organization, but by the Holy Spirit. Often we have used God's glory for our own purposes—to showcase our spiritual gifts and promote our churches.

Jesus said the glory should first of all produce oneness, and then out of that oneness the miracles would flow. That way only the Father receives the glory.

Phillip Keller, author of the well-known book *A Shepherd Looks at Psalm 23*, provides many insights into the relationship between a shepherd and his flock of sheep. As a shepherd himself,

> Often we have used God's glory for our own purposes—to showcase our spiritual gifts and promote our churches.

Phillip learned many valuable things about how sheep operate— things that can be directly applied to Jesus and His sheep, the body of believers in the church.

One thing he points out is that among sheep the order of dominance is called the "butting order." The dominant ewe is usually the source of tension, rivalry, and competition within a flock. But he finally came up with an answer to the troublesome competition factor. Here's what he discovered:

> One point that always interested me very much was that whenever I came into view and my presence attracted their attention, the sheep quickly forgot their foolish rivalries and stopped their fighting. The shepherd's presence made all the difference in their behavior.[1]

The shepherd's presence—this is the answer for us as the body of Christ as well. When we can discern that He is in our midst, then all our petty jealousies and squabbles will dissolve. Joining together to exalt Him in collective praise and worship will do far more than organization, discussion, and programs ever can. Unity is not just a nice fringe benefit of being a Christian. Unity is at the very heart of all that is done in His name. Without it we struggle along in our own strength, accomplishing very little that will last. But with it all the treasures of heaven are ours . . . and the darkness trembles. The Shepherd's presence makes all the difference.

Applying the Lessons

- *Ministerial groups are great if they are focused on Christ. Check the spiritual health of the one in your community and pray, asking God to show you what your response should be. (Keep attending? Politely bow out? Start a new one with other pastors who share your heart?)*

- *With the goal of advancing the kingdom of God, list some ways that the churches in your town or city could work together.*

- *Take some time to discuss what your individual church's function is within the larger plan of God. (Remember the three W's?) Then pray about how your role can be expanded, developed, and used to bless others.*

Discipleship

He will take you where
you do not want to go—
that line you drew
when you said
"this far and no farther."

Otherwise,
all you have accomplished
is to follow your flesh,
your desires,
and narrow knowledge
of Christianity.

It is no longer a line
but a great chasm of fear
that must be crossed
if you are to fight.
You cannot defeat
the supernatural
with your strength
but must rely on Him.

The battle is safe
to those at the back
offering their advice
in ignorance and safety.

You really have no choice.
He warned you about
counting the cost
and you said,
"Praise God, yes!"

Now
He has come to collect.

You must follow Him into battle
without the regret,
If I had only known!
You knew.
He said it would cost your life.

His Answer

This, then, is how you should pray: . . .
"your kingdom come, your will be done on
earth as it is in heaven."
MATTHEW 6:9–10

Our constant prayer as a church for our village was that we would show forth the glory of God, fulfill His purpose for us, and become a "city on a hill" that would draw people by God's light. We had no idea that God would answer those prayers in ways that would cause division even among our church family. We often forget that Jesus warned us about this.

> Do not suppose that I have come to bring peace to the earth. I did not come to bring peace, but a sword. For I have come to turn "a man against his father, a daughter against her mother, a daughter-in-law against her mother-in-law—a man's enemies will be the members of his own household" (Matthew 10:34–36).

Some twenty years ago an African-American family moved into our town. At that time a cross was burned in their front yard and some damage was done to their house. We were shocked at this reaction in South Holland, which prided itself as a "Village of Churches" complete with praying hands on its water tower.

A number of people made sure they welcomed this family and

let them know that this was certainly an isolated incident because we were, after all, a Christian community. Life seemed to go on as usual for a number of years with African-American families continuing to move into our town a few at a time.

But as their overall population slowly grew in our community, we noticed some white families starting to move away—gradually at first, then with accelerating momentum. John and I couldn't believe it. *"White flight" in a Christian community? Impossible!*

Prejudice is never acceptable anywhere, but in our village it seemed unthinkable. In 1850, when the Fugitive Slave Law was enacted, imposing a penalty on anyone aiding the Underground Railroad, First Reformed Church in South Holland acted as a transfer spot for the Railroad. One of the residents also had a "safe house" on his farm. These good Christian people were opposed to the practice of slavery and helped the early Republican abolitionist cause. They even took up collections for Negro education.

The compassion this village showed toward the Negro slave brought an unexpected dividend years later. The South Holland Bank was one of the few banks that didn't close during the Great Depression, and the farmers' vegetable crops were "Depression-proof."

These unusual occurrences don't seem so strange when we remember what Proverbs 19:17 declares: "He who is kind to the poor lends to the Lord, and he will reward him for what he has done." God did reward the descendants of the original settlers by keeping them from poverty during this terrible time in our nation's history.

Now, one hundred fifty years later, South Holland is again providing a safe place for the African-Americans fleeing the dangers of life in the city of Chicago—drugs, gangs, and drive-by shootings. They are attracted by our strong faith-community and our motto that says we are *A Community of Faith, Family, and Future.*

DISCONNECTING FAITH AND LIFE

It was sad for us to realize that some of our fellow believers were blindly following the world's values and giving in to the fears of prejudice. These Christians, who would gladly send money to a missionary in Africa, were unwilling to live next door to an African-American family.

Every Christian espouses the *idea* of unity, but the challenge comes when we have to put that idea into action. The *reality* of unity is that our brothers and sisters in Christ come in all colors and from every socioeconomic

> **These Christians, who would gladly send money to a missionary in Africa, were unwilling to live next door to an African-American family.**

background. We can talk glowingly about reconciliation through Christ, but the world will not be impressed until the church demonstrates it.

Many of the pastors in our community did not encourage their parishioners to stay, and some refused to even mention integration from the pulpit. Some of the people who moved their place of residence drove back every week to attend church, so why make waves? Little did the pastors realize that a person who moves away may return to his home church for two or three years, but after that will likely settle into a congregation closer to his place of residence.

German theologian Dietrich Bonhoeffer recognized this same cowardice among the German pastors during the rise of the Third Reich under Adolph Hitler. One of the leaders in the Confessional Church of Germany, Bonhoeffer implored the pastors to speak out against the growing discrimination against the Jews. But they did not welcome his input. Finally they literally shut him out of their meetings, declaring he was sowing dissention in the church.

It may seem a great leap to compare the persecution of the Jews to refusing to live next door to a man of color, but I believe *it is the same mindset.* I have been amazed at the reasons Christians give for choosing to move. One family with a young child said they were moving because they were concerned about the local high school—something they wouldn't need to face for more than seven years!

Not one person has admitted their move is in response to the blacks who are moving into our community. All of them have logical reasons and explanations for their move while carefully avoiding the word *prejudice*. We all do this in different areas of our lives. The trouble with deception, though, is that we don't fool God—or other people. Most of the time we are only deceiving ourselves.

It is very important that we strive to eliminate anything in our Christian lives that will give the enemy territory from which to work. We cannot afford to allow our theology to get disconnected from our everyday lives. While many of us give lip service to the *idea* of unity as portrayed in Psalm 133, not many want the *reality* of living next door to a person of color. Eleven o'clock on Sunday morning is still the most segregated hour in Christendom.

HIS WILL OR MY WILL?

It took years of praying for our community to bring about God's purpose here, and when His answer came many of us couldn't accept it. The prayer *Your* will be done was changed to *My* will be done.

God has called Christians the "salt of the earth" (Matthew 5:13) because salt is used to enhance flavor and keep food from spoiling. This is the kind of effect He wants us to have on our environment. What we often overlook, though, is the fact that salt must be distributed properly if it is to be effective for either of these purposes. As salt, Christians need to be strategically placed by God where our corruption-restraining and flavor-enhancing properties are most needed. I believe that *where* we are in the world is almost as important to God as *who* we are.

I learned this early on in my Christian walk because I was having a hard time accepting South Holland as my permanent home. This suburb of Chicago is very close to Gary, Indiana, a town that at that time had several steel mills belching out massive quantities of environmental pollution. Every time the wind blew in a westerly direction I could smell the mills and my desire to move grew exponentially. My husband and I shared a dream of moving out west some day. The uncluttered landscape and wide-open, unpolluted skies seemed to beckon me with every westerly wind.

I finally had a revelation from God: I had never given Him the right to choose where I would live. So one night, after a lot of mental struggle, I yielded up my dream of moving to Colorado. Soon after that, John and I prayed together and accepted South Holland as God's choice for us. This was where He wanted us to live during our sojourn on this earth. So, unless He shows us otherwise, we will remain here.

It is amazing what happens when you embrace the will of God. The mills were still pumping out their poisonous gasses, but it no longer bothered me. I knew that God could protect my lungs in any environment. As a bonus, a long-standing sinus problem I had been battling was healed even in the midst of one of the worst areas in the nation for sinus problems.

Many people do not give God the option to decide their place of residence. So they run. To handle the "white flight," many areas are mushrooming with new home developments. Over the state line in Indiana, areas that were once considered one-horse towns are now sprouting half-million-dollar home developments. The hemorrhaging continues even now.

One day I had a doctor's appointment in one of those fast-growing suburbs. As I drove by the sparkling new homes and beautiful parks, I understood the draw these areas had for the white suburbanite. All around me were young families and their children—bike riding on the new bike trails, pushing their babies on swings in their wonderfully manicured parks, or just strolling down the sidewalk. Most noticeably, there was not a black face in the whole area.

Spiritual Eyes

I was reminded of the story of Abraham and Lot in Genesis 13. Abraham, against the Lord's command, took his nephew Lot with him when he left his country, people, and father's household. But in spite of his disobedience in this one point God still blessed Abraham abundantly. So much so that the land could no longer support all of their combined flocks, herds, and dwellings. After quarreling erupted between their herdsmen, Abraham suggested they separate and graciously told Lot:

> Let's not have any quarreling between you and me, or between your herdsmen and mine, for we are brothers. Is not the whole land before you? Let's part company. If you go to the left, I'll go to the right; if you go to the right, I'll go to the left. (Genesis 13:8–9)

Abraham had learned something in his travels: He would come out best if *God made the choice for him.* Lot had not learned this; he was still driven by the lust of the eye.

> Lot looked up and saw that the whole plain of the Jordan was well watered, like the garden of the Lord, like the land of Egypt, toward Zoar. . . . So Lot *chose for himself* the whole plain of the Jordan and set out toward the east. The two men parted company. (Genesis 13:10–11)

Lot looked with his physical eyes and made a decision about where he would live, while Scripture says that Abraham was "looking forward to the city with foundations, whose architect and builder is God" (Hebrews 11:10). In other words, Abraham saw things with "spiritual eyes" and recognized that it is more important to enjoy God's fellowship than to partake of anything the world has to offer. Abraham realized that wherever he settled it was not his final destination. It was only a temporary dwelling where he could do the will of God.

What does it matter, then, where we live? Many people spend their whole lives dedicated to their house, continually redecorating, enlarging, digging their tent pegs deeper and deeper into this miry clay, rather than seeing it only as a stopgap on our pilgrim journey. Like Abraham, our hearts should be set on the city to come (Hebrews 13:14), not our temporary home here on earth. We can all eagerly await the home in heaven that Jesus has gone to prepare for us.

Once I realized that I could do the will of God only in the place He has assigned to me, my perspective totally changed. When the racial population changed in our town, it didn't matter because *I knew this was where God wanted me.*

White Americans are used to being the dominant population in this nation, but that is slowly changing. According to the latest

U.S. Census Bureau estimates, 4.5 million children under the age of eighteen are now multiracial. The rate of interracial marriages is skyrocketing. In some areas, one in six babies being born is of two or more racial heritages—making multiracial youth one of the fastest-growing segments of our population.[1]

In light of these statistics, the church can no longer afford to tolerate racial prejudice or espouse a "separate but equal" mindset. Isolating ourselves from those we deem of lower status in society or treating them differently is not acceptable Christian behavior— God makes this clear in Scripture (James 2:1–9; 1 John 4:20; 1 Timothy 5:21; Leviticus 19:15). If the church is going to have any impact on our society, then we must reflect that society. We must mirror the multicultural world around us and repent of racist attitudes and false generalizations about different ethnic groups.

I have heard some people rationalize their move because they are afraid that we will have more crime in our village because of the growth of the African-American population. Yet our recent statistics do not support that fear—our crime rate actually went down after they moved in! It is not the population that determines the crime rate, but the prayers of God's people.

Also, many were concerned about the value of their homes. Again, this fear has proved to be false. Our homes in South Holland have skyrocketed in value, with rates up 6 percent annually. In contrast, a once affluent suburb to the south has experienced declining real estate values. In many cases white Christians are running from invalid assumptions and lies of the enemy. It is so important that we seek God to determine whether our decision to move is from Him or not. Again, we need to ask: Is this His will or my will?

UNITY DEMONSTRATED

We do have a committed group of people in our village who desire integration and want to see Christian unity demonstrated in a new way. A former Young Life leader, Wayne Van Swol is an elder at First Reformed Church. While on a recent vacation, God woke him in the early morning hours and told him that He had chosen South Holland to become a "city on a hill" that would draw many people.

Wayne was so impacted by this message that he shares it wherever he goes, and he is living the message too. He built a new home for his family just a block from us. Many people look at him as if he's crazy to build a new home in a village where the African-American population is about 75 percent. But Wayne has the "eyes of faith" that Abraham had. He knows what God has done in this village and what He is about to do. He doesn't want to miss out on his own calling and the plan and purposes of God.

I am always stunned by the reaction of people when I tell them I live in South Holland. They blink once or twice, and then the more aggressive ones ask me when I am going to move. They cannot imagine why I would *choose* to live as a minority in our village. Most of these people are not aware that many of the African-Americans that have moved into our village are professional people and the majority of them are committed Christians. So they look at me as if I have lost my mind.

The Work of Faith

Faith is always strange to those living in unbelief. The eyes of faith see God at work while those with earthly vision only see the circumstances. I often think of Noah, who labored for about one hundred years building a structure he had never seen before to protect his family from a coming flood that no one had ever experienced.

The Bible calls faith a "work" (2 Thessalonians 1:11 KJV), and it often does require a lot of work to stand true to the vision God has given us in spite of all the arrows of unbelief aimed at our hearts.

Many of us at Spirit of God Fellowship have experienced deep grief as we watched people we have loved and nurtured leave for greener pastures. With each new pronouncement the devil seems to attack with renewed doubt. *Should we just leave too? Maybe our vision of a "city on a hill" will never come true. Maybe we are pathetic dreamers drunk with our own dreams.*

But then the blessed Holy Spirit renews the vision in our

hearts through His Word, or a song, or a radio preacher. Like Noah, we pick up our hammers to build something no one has ever seen before except through the eyes of faith.

Since our many ministries function mainly through our volunteers, it is difficult to see our church becoming smaller. Yet the Lord continually reminds us of one of the greatest victories in the Bible—when Gideon defeated the Midianites against overwhelming odds (Judges 7).

In an amazing statement God told Gideon that he had *too many* men for Him to deliver Midian into their hands. *Too many men!* Imagine any army general today giving this directive to his troops. He would be laughed out of service. But God knew that the large number of men would claim they had won the victory and refuse to give Him the glory for it.

God weeded the men out in two steps. First, He told the fearful to leave. "So twenty-two thousand men left, while ten thousand remained" (Judges 7:3). With two-thirds of his army gone, Gideon must have been wondering if God was planning some suicide mission for them. Then to his great dismay, God told him, "There are still too many men" (Judges 7:4). He gave Gideon a strange directive.

> So Gideon took the men down to the water. There the Lord told him, "Separate those who lap the water with their tongues like a dog from those who kneel down to drink." Three hundred men lapped with their hands to their mouths. All the rest got down on their knees to drink. (Judges 7:5–6)

Gideon was left with only three hundred men out of the original thirty-two thousand! That's about 1 percent. Those three hundred who brought their hand up to their mouth to drink were those who kept their eye on the vision even while occupied with daily pursuits.

At our church we noticed the same type of pruning going on in our congregation. First, those who were fearful because of the changes in their neighborhoods left en masse. Then there was a period when the village and the church seemed to stabilize. Eventually, though, people began moving again. We were surprised to see solidly committed Christians who truly loved the Lord making the decision to move. We couldn't really figure out all the reasons, of course. But to us it seemed like their focus was on the cares of this life—jobs, property values, schools, new homes—rather than the vision we had all shared for our village.

The Bible asks the question: "Can two walk together, except they be agreed?" (Amos 3:3 KJV). It is amazing how long you can know a Christian brother and sister and think that they see what you do and are walking in the light of the same vision. But sometimes we are deceived by outward appearances. Even though John regularly taught God's vision for our church from the pulpit there were some who had never embraced it themselves.

A vision from God has to be received by revelation to our spirit. That's why those who tried to perceive it through their minds never truly apprehended it. They couldn't see that *the changing racial profile of our village was a direct answer* to the prayers we had offered for so many years. Those of us who remained had to remind ourselves that the same God who birthed our church thirty-four years ago was now pruning us so we would be more fruitful.

THE REWARDS ARE WORTH IT

At one time South Holland was the onion set capital of the world. Farmers produced small mature bulbs called onion sets that were sold and planted the following year by home gardeners, truck farmers, and commercial onion growers. These early onion set growers faced many obstacles in their developing industry. An amusing anecdote about their struggle gives hope and encouragement to us as we undergo our own struggles in the village.

> He had to stand up to the amused skepticism of his American neighbors; and worse yet, of grain or corn-growing Hollanders. To try to make anything out of that swamp! It was a laugh! Grubbing on hands and knees in the black ooze—who but a fool would think of such a thing? And later, when a few square yards had actually been cleared for a crop, to crawl ant-like over the ground setting each individual plant with his fin-

gers, pressing down the muck around it—a man must be balmy to do such a thing.

Later—years later—many of those same fools might overtake the skeptics walking along the country highway, threadbare and unable to afford even a horse—overtake them in an eight-cylinder Buick and give them a lift to town. But that fact did not help them in the early days when they had only faith and shrewd Dutch common sense to keep them going.[2]

Just as the Dutch farmer on his hands and knees in the black muck had to press each individual onion plant in the ground, impacting our community is a messy process too. It requires our spending a lot of time on our knees, praying and interceding. Are we like that Dutch farmer, willing to patiently sow and tend each tiny plant for however long it takes, denying ourselves the leisure time we all think we deserve?

We have sown good seed in our village for thirty-four years through prayer and community involvement, and we are still waiting for the harvest. It will come, we have no doubt, because God's Word cannot return empty—it will accomplish what He desires (Isaiah 55:11).

We have been tested by disappointment, failure, heartache, fear, and doubt. But through it all, something within testifies to *keep on keeping on.* "Though it tarry, wait for it; because it will surely come, it will not tarry" (Habakkuk 2:3b KJV).

No Quick Fixes

Christians in America have been taught that there is a perfect prayer that will bind every demon oppressing us, holiness is achievable overnight, and there are seven steps to receiving a healing; they've been told how an instant financial breakthrough will undo years of indulgent living, or a sizable donation to a ministry will bring the answer in the form of a prayer cloth sent to your door. We like instant food and instant deliverance.

But Americans are waking up. We are beginning to realize that fast food is fake food and harmful to one's heart. And so are the fast answers being pumped out by today's drive-through ministries. Eventually our hearts become clogged with half-truths and quick fixes that lead only to disappointment and disaster.

Listening to many of today's preachers it seems that all we need to win battles is the right mindset: Just believe. An arrogant attitude and loud voice also help. But Paul, the greatest of the apostles, taught no such quick fixes. In a passage in 2 Corinthians he lists the unusual path to spiritual success:

> As servants of God we commend ourselves . . . in great endurance; in troubles, hardships and distresses; in beatings, imprisonments and riots; in hard work, sleepless nights and hunger; in purity, understanding, patience and kindness; in the Holy Spirit and in sincere love; in truthful speech and in the power of God; with weapons of righteousness in the right hand and in the left; through glory and dishonor, bad report and good report; genuine, yet regarded as impostors; known, yet regarded as unknown; dying, and yet we live on; beaten, and yet not killed; sorrowful, yet always rejoicing; poor, yet making many rich; having nothing, and yet possessing everything. (2 Corinthians 6:4–10)

Given this list of qualifications to follow Jesus, how many today would choose to do so? Paul begins this passage saying he didn't want to put a stumbling block in anyone's path. He knew that half-truths about the cost of becoming a Christian would eventually trip up those who thought it was all about a "me-centered" gospel.

Like those early Dutch onion farmers, our congregation has been called fools, and we've even thought that about ourselves in our weaker, private moments. *What can so few do against the giants of greed, denominationalism, and racial prejudice—terrifying creatures—as we stand with our few stones and a slingshot?* It has been hard work, sometimes backbreaking and discouraging work, to attempt to bring unity to churches and to an entire community.

The enemy is too strong! I've lamented many times. Then I remember . . . the enemy has already been defeated; all we have to do is enforce the victory won at Calvary! Unity is the purpose of God, the representation on earth of the Godhead, and the final prayer of Jesus. So how can we lose?

Applying the Lessons

- If racial prejudice is an issue in your community, pray about how your church can take a stand against it. Then boldly enact what God shows you.

- Sharing on a regular basis the unique vision of your church is important in ensuring that members are "agreed" as they serve together. Plan how to keep the vision before all the people, whether they are newcomers to the church or people who have been there for many years.

- Come against the "quick fixes" that are being taught in some circles. Model and teach the discipline and hard work that always accompany a faith walk with God.

Two Masters

When did I become Lord?
In a sudden, angry moment?
I would have noticed.
It happened slowly, insidiously,
my rise to ruler of my life.
I forgot my commission
from Him, who took towel and basin
then told us to go and do likewise.
When did I stop looking
for feet to wash
and look instead
for feet to follow me?
Helping me attain my goals.
When did I tire of losing my life?

Perhaps it is that ever-present,
selfish nature within me
that responds to weariness
and discouragement
by asserting itself,
telling me I deserve it.

His way is so unlike mine.
He counts my loss a victory,
My weakness—strength,
And my lack—His gain.
My mind's transformation
is not yet complete;
those ideas are still strange . . . foreign.
Still, my spirit bears witness to their truth.
So I will once again
take up towel and basin
and stoop to wash the feet of those
He has entrusted to me,
for I am a servant and there can be only
one Lord.

Touching People, Touching God

The man who really counts in the world is the doer, not the mere critic—the man who actually does the work, even if roughly and imperfectly, not the man who only talks or writes about how it ought to be done.

THEODORE ROOSEVELT

Ministry to drug addicts continues to be our primary outreach. The state drug program is great at detoxing addicts and providing a substitute drug called methadone to help them kick heroin. They also present many behavior modification courses that help the addicts look at negative behavior patterns in their lives. However, the state's entire effort concentrates on externals. It cannot deal with the heart, which is the ultimate problem with addicts.

The Bible studies we present at the state drug center concentrate on man's need for a savior. When we were invited into this facility, the director told us, "We need all the help we can get. Our recidivism rate is about 95 percent." It is amazing how eager many public facilities are to have faith-based ministries help them because they know they are not getting the job done.

On the negative side he also told us, "You won't last here." When asked why he would say that he replied, "Christian groups never do." What a sad commentary.

Out of this ministry we established both Harvey House for

men and Tabitha House for women. They provide a setting where former addicts can learn the principles of the kingdom and how to live as Christian men and women. As I mentioned in chapter 9, we established these homes in the city of Harvey, located on the south side of Chicago. We saw the hopelessness of the people as wonderfully fertile ground for sharing the gospel.

SERVING THE COMMUNITY IN HIS NAME

One of the first outreaches we established in our community—in July 1990—was a food pantry. We knew there was a need for emergency food, and we hoped it would also serve to draw people to Harvey House. We started out purchasing food to give out to people in extreme situations. However, we soon found out that the Greater Chicago Food Depository helps small community pantries like ours. We established Monday nights as a time when people in the neighborhood could come and receive much-needed groceries.

We may not think our community has a "hunger issue," but today hunger has a new face. It includes "single mothers stuck in low wage jobs, married couples who can't keep up with soaring housing costs, and able-bodied people who can't find jobs."[1] This need creates a wonderful opportunity for the church to touch lives with the gospel by taking action. Helping people tangibly by meeting critical physical needs in their lives tells them "we care about you" in a way no amount of words can convey.

> Suppose a brother or sister is without clothes and daily food. If one of you says to him, "Go, I wish you well; keep warm and well fed," but does nothing about his physical needs, what good is it? In the same way, faith by itself, if it is not accompanied by action, is dead. (James 2:15–17)

Too often we have mouthed placebos such as *I will pray for you* to soothe our conscience, but we have not been the hands of Christ to help the one in need. Even worse, the poor have at times been taken advantage of by prosperity teachers who dangle the carrot of success before them while lining their own pockets with offerings. No wonder many of the poor are cynical about religion and preachers.

A pastor from Detroit who heard about our ministries, Jim Bennethum, came for a visit and tour of Restoration Ministries. Thankfully, he went back home with a desire to reach out to the poor. God directed Jim and his church leaders to visit the homeless on the street every Saturday and give them sandwiches and clothing. While there, they asked the people they met if they could pray with them. They also inquired about other needs they might have.

One homeless man always stood on the same overpass with a sign that read: Homeless, Hungry, God Bless. Jim made sure he stopped every week to give him food and talk to him. He soon found out that this man—Mike Acquaviva—lived under that bridge; it had been his place of residence for twelve years. Eventually Mike gave his life to Jesus, and soon after Jim brought him to our men's home, Harvey House. Today Mike is the resident director in charge of the other men.

Just like Jim, God will guide and direct any Christian whose heart is willing to reach out to serve the poor. The needy come in all sorts of packages. Sometimes they show themselves as a man standing on a street corner begging, a widow who is deep in despair, or a confused teen who needs someone to talk to. Whatever the case may be, our ministry to them must begin with a heart that is so thankful to God for our salvation that *we are compelled* to serve others. Paul put it this way: "For the love of Christ controls and urges and impels us" (2 Corinthians 5:14 AMP).

Soon after we began the food pantry, John had an idea for a related program called *Bread of Life*. We went around to supermarkets and grocery stores, asking them if they would donate their day-old bread and pastries to our ministry. It is amazing how many responded. Soon community residents could come to our pantry every day from three to five in the afternoon to receive a bag of baked goods.

This program ran for six years. At its peak we were supplying seventy-five ministries with bakery products. This meant that we had trucks running day and night to pick up and deliver all the goods. It was a huge investment of time and volunteers.

Out of the food pantry and *Bread of Life* program we developed a seniors ministry. Many senior citizens are homebound, either because of a limiting physical condition or fear of crime. We decided to deliver food and bakery products to needy seniors as one aspect of our ministry to them.

A volunteer would sign up to deliver to two seniors whose names we obtained from the food pantry or from the Harvey YMCA. Then we encouraged the whole family to get involved in visiting the seniors assigned to them. It is life-changing for children of all ages to be involved with helping someone in need. They learn even at an early age the blessing we receive when we follow Jesus' command to "Give, and it will be given to you" (Luke 6:38). It also promotes a grateful attitude in them when they see that many people in the world don't have the basics of life that they take for granted.

Kids Make Great Servants

My oldest granddaughter, Nina, has been going to Harvey House with her mother for years. There are many little chores that children can do there to help out, and all the time they are learning to be servants. It sets the stage for what God wants them to do when they grow up.

Servanthood needs to be modeled, because our flesh rebels at the very thought of it. Sure, kids have to learn to serve in their home too, but serving others outside their own family and seeing the smiles of thanks is a great boost. The children in our congregation love to be involved with the different aspects of serving, like setting the tables for the banquets we hold at the church building.

One other advantage that comes out of children's involvement with the poor is that they lose their fear of urban decay—boarded up homes, unkempt yards, bag ladies, gang bangers, sullen expressions. In time they come to see this setting as an *opportunity* for ministry rather than a place to be avoided.

Adults who serve as models for children often think this way. They wait for the "sinners" from impoverished neighborhoods to come into the church if they want help. But people like John Wesley were successful because they were willing *to go to the people* to offer help. One biographer of Wesley said, he "looked at the same miserable conditions and saw a situation which was ripe for evangelism."[2]

Service to the poor also curtails one of the greatest cancers of the church—judgmentalism. Parents and children both begin to understand the hopelessness of poverty rather than falling back on trite clichés such as "Well, if they wanted to work they could find a job."

After six years the *Bread of Life* program was so successful in supplying bread, bakery goods, and even produce that most of our time was involved in picking up and distributing the products. This huge time commitment was presenting a problem because another ministry need was also vying for our attention: the children.

GOD'S HEART FOR CHILDREN

In this decaying suburb many children come from single-parent homes, and Mom is often a crack addict who works as a prostitute to support her habit. Or perhaps the children live with a caring but overburdened grandmother who just doesn't have the time or energy to give them the support they need.

As more and more children began "hanging out" at Harvey House, seeking the love and attention they were missing out on at home, we knew that we had to do something. We kept the food pantry going, but closed down the enormously time-consuming *Bread of Life* program. In this way we had more time to devote to developing needed children's programs.

We began a Friday afternoon Kids Club to instruct these children in the Bible. Out of this flowed many ministries, which included tutoring, homework help, computer club, and Kids Café. At the end of our first year of Kids Club we decided to have a vacation Bible school, and about one hundred children attended. On Saturday, after VBS was over, we sponsored a neighborhood block party. We had everything from a petting zoo to small rides for the kids and plenty of hamburgers, hot dogs, and other goodies for everybody. We were astounded when about eight hundred Harvey residents showed up for the party.

One week later we received the tragic news that one of the children who attended VBS had died in a drowning accident at a local pool. Our grief was mingled with joy, though, when we discovered a cross she had made. On the back was her childish prayer asking Jesus to come into her heart. Her mother asked us to share at the funeral and to read her prayer. Great shouts of *Hallelujah!* and *Praise God!* punctuated our reading. These shouts seemed to be the answer we were seeking about whether to continue this ministry.

Our children's ministries all function under the umbrella of *Project Intercept*, a gang prevention program. We are always looking for new ways to win the youth of our town to Christ and distance them from drugs and gangs. Our newest program, the *Harvey Boxing Club*, came about quite by accident.

Nate came to Harvey House from the state drug center. Both his mother and father were drug addicted and he was one of the youngest of the large family. As a child, he had discovered boxing as a way to escape his home situation, and he had eventually become a Golden Gloves amateur boxer. One day he was sparring with another man in the alley behind Harvey House. It wasn't long before a crowd of young boys gathered around, all asking the same question: "Can you teach us to box?"

When Nate told John about the incident, John immediately recognized a "golden" opportunity and began to search out a place to have a boxing club. The mayor of Harvey donated the old police garage, and after raising four hundred and fifty thousand dollars, we had not only our boxing club but also *Gallery of the Arts*, a place where students learn painting, sculpting, and other art forms. Training in drama, set building, and stage production is also available.

Last summer we trained sixty young boys and girls in the rigorous discipline of boxing. Boxing is a proven delinquency deterrent. We have found that their grades improve too because they must maintain a certain grade point average to continue with the program. Still another bonus of the program is that the kids are exposed to ethnic diversity in the club, something many from poor neighborhoods never experience.

Nate prays with the boxers before and after training sessions and matches. At the end of each day they have a sharing time to discuss the practical challenges they are facing each day. They are directed to spiritual principles from the Bible as the way to deal with their problems.

We have had the opportunity to host four international events and two Illinois state matches. We have won thirteen Illinois state Silver Gloves, four Illinois state Junior Olympics, and we have two national champions—a fifteen-year-old girl and a ten-year-old boy. We have had the first-place team in state for three years running. But the best part is that we have made contacts with so many young people, many of whom are unchurched.

In the appendix at the end of the book I list the thirty current endeavors of Restoration Ministries. These are always expanding as we think of new ways to touch people. We have several of our ex-Harvey House men employed by a local nursing home. They use their job to share the gospel with these desperately sick and lonely people. They also bring them to our Senior Banquets, which we hold at the church twice a year.

LOVE IN ACTION

There are so many ways to reach the unchurched, and all it takes is a desire to share Christ. Francis of Assisi (1181–1226) is accredited with saying, "Preach the gospel all the time; if necessary use words." This is good advice, because people in this nation are word-hardened and no longer listen to spiritual jargon. They do, however, respond to *love in action*. We are only limited in the scope of our ministries by our lack of imagination and motivation.

Many Christians today are lone rangers, interested only in their own personal agenda. They don't think about the responsibility we have been given for the welfare of others—that we are our brother's keeper. Francis Schaeffer said some years ago that we are a post-Christian society, resulting in many Christians drawing their circles tighter and wrapping their doctrinal blankets around themselves to keep out the big bad world.

Charles Colson declares: "Only when we see our faith as an all-encompassing life system that vigorously brings hope and redemption to every arena will we have an effect on reversing the prevailing cultural tides and resist the accommodation that can so easily ensnare us."[3]

The Coming Separation

The parable of the last judgment in Matthew 25 is one of the most vivid stories told by Jesus. It follows the second coming parables in Matthew 24 and 25, which began on the Mount of Olives when the disciples asked Jesus these questions: "When will this happen, and what will be the sign of your coming and of the end of the age?" (Matthew 24:3). This story about the last judgment is the climax of those parables and reveals the Son of Man coming in glory and sitting on the throne as the judge of all nations.

At first all the people are herded together before Him. Then He begins to separate them as a shepherd separates the sheep from the goats. Surprisingly, the separation here is not based on knowledge of the great doctrines of the faith, fasting, prayers, paying tithes, church attendance, or stunning testimonies, but on *simple acts of kindness done for those in need.*

> Then the King will say to those on his right, "Come, you who are blessed by my Father; take your inheritance, the kingdom prepared for you since the creation of the world. For I was hungry and you gave me something to eat, I was thirsty and you gave me something to drink, I was a stranger and you invited me in. I needed clothes and you clothed me, I was sick and you looked after me, I was in prison and you came to visit me." Then the righteous will answer him, "Lord, when did we see you hungry and feed you, or thirsty and give you something to drink? When did we see you a stranger and invite you in, or needing clothes and clothe you? When did we see you sick or in prison and go to visit you?" Then the King will reply, "I tell you the truth, whatever you did for one of the least of these brothers of mine, you did for me." Then he will say to

those on his left, "Depart from me, you who are cursed, into the eternal fire prepared for the devil and his angels. For I was hungry and you gave me nothing to eat, I was thirsty and you gave me nothing to drink, I was a stranger and you did not invite me in, I needed clothes and you did not clothe me, I was sick and in prison and you did not look after me." They also will answer, "Lord, when did we see you hungry or thirsty or a stranger or needing clothes or sick or in prison, and did not help you?" He will reply, "I tell you the truth, whatever you *did not do* for one of the least of these, you did not do for me." Then they will go away to eternal punishment, but the righteous to eternal life. (Matthew 25:34–46)

Evidence of Our Faith

These verses have elicited major theological debate but I prefer to look at them, with fear and awe, as the King's own description of judgment. The Lord spoke this only three days before His sufferings, and to men He loved deeply. I don't believe Jesus was giving them theological fodder, but was warning them—and all of us who would follow Him—that there will be a judgment based on our treatment of others in need.

First, the King reminds the sheep of all their works of charity toward the "least of these," and we might be tempted to surmise from this that salvation is a result of good works. But from many New Testament passages we know that this is a wrong assumption. Rather than the *means of salvation*, good works serve as the *evidence for genuine faith* in Christ. As James says, "I will show you my faith by what I do" (James 2:18).

Going back to the passage in Matthew 25, we see that the people who performed the acts of kindness thought they were doing them for other people, but Jesus tells them that the acts were actually done for the King himself. They are surprised and cry out, *When did we see you?*

> When the saints stand before the judgment seat, the bare thought of there being any excellence in what they have done will be new to them, for they have formed a very lowly estimate of their own performances. They fed the hungry, clothed the naked, visited the sick, for Christ's sake, because it was the

sweetest thing in the world to do anything for Jesus. They did it because they delighted to do it, because they could not help doing it, because their new nature impelled them to do it.[4]

This, of course, is the key to all service for God. It is not that we serve out of a sullen obedience, like a child asked to do a chore he dislikes. Rather, we serve because we can't help it—our new nature impels us. When we love someone we do not serve them out of a sense of duty, but joy.

Some might not believe me, but the highlight of my week is my Monday night Bible study at the state drug center. Of course, there are those evenings when I am tired and look at my lounge chair longingly, but I go because of my commitment to Jesus. Then, something happens when I arrive—I am energized and filled with joy because that is the place God has assigned for me to serve. Surprisingly, it is not difficult; in fact, I am no longer tired when I finish up and usually have to be dragged out of there as I linger to pray for "just one more person."

How wonderful it is when each of us finds that one thing we have been created to do with joy. It may be visiting the sick, teaching children, volunteering at a food pantry, orphanage, or shelter, baby-sitting for a single mom, driving a senior citizen to the doctor, building homes for Habitat for Humanity . . . the list is endless.

> **It is often the little, hidden kindnesses done out of love for Jesus that yield the great returns in this life and for eternity.**

Some of these may seem like small things, but Teresa of Avila (1515–1582) said, "Our Lord does not care so much for the importance of our works as for the love with which they are done." It is often the little, hidden kindnesses done out of love for Jesus that yield the great returns in this life and for eternity.

In the end it won't matter what wonderful prophecies we spoke, how many times we gave a message in tongues, or how many mysteries of God we revealed in our bestselling book, if it was all about our ego. Working with the "least of these" has no ego-building perks; often what is done is unseen and unappreciated.

REMINDERS OF GOD'S GRACE

Christianity is about people, and touching people is touching God who created them. What I dislike most about writing is that I lose contact with the people who remind me of God's love and grace. There is a built-in bonus with the poor—serving them doesn't build our egos but it does build up our faith in God.

As I see the grace God gives to the addict who falls again and again, I am reminded of the grace He gives me daily. As God uses our ministry to help the poor, I remember that Jesus exhorted me to not worry about what I will eat or drink, and my faith in His provision is increased. As I feel His love pour through me to the disadvantaged, I am transported back to that first-love experience when Christ found me in my weakness. Some Christians feel that the addict doesn't deserve help, but then *neither do any of us.*

I can remember many nights when I would drive out to Brandon House to minister to the drug addicts there, while my own son, Tom, was trapped in cocaine addiction. Often I would think, *God, how can I help these people when my own son is an addict?*

God seemed to say through my thoughts, *You minister to these, and I will minister to your son.* Miraculously, whenever I left Brandon House my faith for Tom's deliverance was renewed. And yes, eventually Tom was delivered from his addictions in a powerful and supernatural way.

Jeremiah the prophet declared: "'He defended the cause of the poor and needy, and *so all went well.* Is that not what it means to know me?' declares the Lord" (Jeremiah 22:16).

What a powerful statement: "Is that not what it means to know me?" To know God is to defend the poor and needy, and if we are obedient to this call, all will go well with us. That doesn't mean that we will always be "healthy, wealthy, and wise." It *does* mean that the really important things, both here in this life and eternally, will go well — and in the end that is all that matters.

But who are the poor and needy? Who is my neighbor that I

am commanded to love *as I love myself?* In response to such a question, Jesus told the parable about the good Samaritan. Our neighbor is essentially any needy person that God puts in our path. Saint Augustine (354-430) gave wise advice on this point: "Since you cannot do good to all, you are to pay special attention to those who, by accidents of time, or place, or circumstance, are brought into closer connection with you."

Each person and each church congregation has an assignment from God. We were created "to do good works, which God prepared in advance for us to do"(Ephesians 2:10). Our assignment has already been prepared so we need to seek God in prayer and then do the thing He puts in our path. It may be only a small kindness, but it may be the doorway into a unique calling.

You Have to Give It Away

As I was thinking about how to end this chapter, I took a break and clicked on a Christian television network. A very well-known Bible teacher was expounding on her latest study. She mentioned that most Christians have a hard time believing that God loves them. She then went on to promote her Bible study that would help them understand how much God loves them.

As I've mentioned, I love to study the Word of God and have been encouraged and blessed often in my devotions. But if our relationship with God is only academic we will never be convinced of His love for us. The addicts have an expression they often use: *To keep it [sobriety] you have to give it away.*

The same is true of God's love. As we give it away to others God constantly fills us with more, and not just a little more . . . but "running over" more. Jesus told us that "with the measure you use, it will be measured to you" (Luke 6:38).

With the measure I use? I guess that means that if I want to experience God's love, I need to pour myself out to others in extravagance. I need to see every person I meet as an opportunity to give out the love of God and thereby glorify Him.

People with true servant hearts know this. Though they may be perceived by the world as rather common and lowly, this characteristic of humility enables them to be channels for pouring out

God's love to others. Into the low places of their lives God's love flows, like water, filling up those low places to overflowing.

That's why those who serve others can experience joy no matter how bad their own circumstances may be. By touching others we actually touch God and know both His presence and His pleasure. Can you think of a higher calling than that?

Applying the Lessons

- *With your church's unique vision from God in mind, design some volunteer ministries that can serve the "hungry, thirsty, sick, and imprisoned" in your community.*

- *Be on the lookout for new ministry opportunities that may come out of casual conversations (like the boxing ministry for kids did).*

- *Don't let a handful of "servants" from your church do all the work! Spread the blessing around by encouraging participation from children, new converts, etc., whenever possible.*

Freedom

I yield my freedom so reluctantly,
like feathers plucked one at a time.
I pull away,
the pain a surprise
(shouldn't sacrifice bring joy?)

    I know I gave you
full surrender
(I remember);
words gushed out
in a moment of revelation,
rethought in harsh reality of daily life
(It's not what I thought it would be)
And what do I do now,
now that I know the truth?

    Covenant does not consider
tender emotions, nor hesitate
to extract the promise.
(In spite of cries of wounded self)
I thought I died with Him
Then why does this flesh protest
at each urging of His Holy Spirit
to give beyond what I am able?

    I thought I was deserving;
logic dictates certain boundaries,
after all. But He is deaf
to my protestations,
and relentless in His quest of quills.
I have no choice
in spite of free will,
for grace does not fight fair.

All arguments are pointless
and absurd.
(It is a language I do not understand)
I am so afraid of yielding
to one who freely,
joyfully surrendered (yielded).
I now see, when He is done,
the "me" I know will be no more.

13 A Tale of Two Women: A Modern-Day Parable of the Church

The first woman was born to wealthy parents in England. Because England still had a monarchy, this little girl often dreamed of being a princess. I suppose that most little girls, at one time or another, think of becoming a princess. But this little girl was the one in a million who actually achieved that dream.

She was a beautiful and gracious princess, and the common people loved her. Her days were exciting and full. When she woke each morning, she would decide what to do that day—you see, her days were her own, to use as she wished. She would buy lovely clothes for all the parties and functions she attended. She would yacht in the blue ocean, play tennis on green grass courts, and drink tea on a beautiful terrace. Many people—some rich and important—desired to spend time with her. It was a beautiful life, and she lived it to the full.

But a princess also has duties. There were expectations placed upon her to bridge the gap between the privileged and the poor, between the blessed and the struggling. So she would also journey out among the common people at times, visiting hospitals, orphanages, AIDS centers, and homeless shelters. Seeing the pain and suffering would bring tears to the eyes of the princess. She would talk, console, hug the children . . . and the people loved her even more. She made such a beautiful picture in her designer suit and saucy little hairdo, leaning over an AIDS victim and comforting him. No wonder the press refused to leave her alone.

Dressed in the rich clothes of a princess, manicured and fussed over like a princess, she was a truly beautiful lady, regal and perfect. The people both loved and envied her. At the end of the day she would return to her castle, far away from the pain and suffering she had witnessed. The guards, security cameras, and large fences made sure that she was safe from the outside world.

Like so many other princesses, she did not want the common people to get too close to her. She liked to mingle among them and do her good deeds, but her interactions were always on her own terms. She didn't want them to get too close, close enough to see her flaws and make her common too.

Even in the best of circumstances a princess can be unhappy. Since her prince could not make her happy, she found someone who could. It was a scandal to the media, who were obsessed with the princess, but even this did not diminish the love lavished upon her by the common people.

Little girls still dreamed of being like her. She could do no wrong. She was young, rich, and beautiful—one of the rare few who could truly have *anything*. She was in complete control of her world . . . except for one thing.

Even a princess cannot control her fate, her time on earth. No amount of money, power, or beauty can change these things. Like so many of the young, she thought she had a lot of time. But something suddenly took away her future and her life. A tragic accident killed both the princess and her lover, the one who made her happy. Some of her last words, yelled to the cameramen who followed her everywhere, were "Leave me alone!"[1]

There was another woman who was also born to wealthy parents. Even though she loved her family and her home, she began at a young age to feel that God was calling her to another kind of life—the life of a servant among people in the poorest country in the world. This young girl, unlike others, did not dream of being a princess. Instead, her dream was to help the hurting and suffering in a faraway land.

With her family background this idea seemed absurd to those around her. Her family had their own dreams and plans for her; they were surprised and shocked that their little girl seemed to want so little in her life. But she knew that God had spoken, so she left her family to follow Him.

She went to live in a home with other servants who felt the same calling. She spent her time there teaching and learning to serve, something that made her content. But even in her contentment she felt there was still something missing. One day, while riding on a train, she looked out the window and suddenly saw it. At once she knew—this was what she had been called to do.[2]

Out the window she saw many people who were desperately poor and ill. She saw them lying in the streets as the train rumbled on. They were naked and filthy, and many of them looked close to death. Would they die right there on the filthy streets? *These are the ones*, God seemed to say, and her spirit soared because she knew she had finally found them—the ones she wanted to help and serve.

She asked to be released from her present duties so she could begin her new life of service. Her superiors gave her leave because they knew she had a vision, a calling from God. As she began His new work for her she was filled not only with contentment but also joy.

The little room where she set up her work was soon filled with desperate people who had no one else to help them. She was so busy that she did not have time to worry about her own needs or comfort, the everyday things, like clothes, food, and drink; she trusted God to provide, and He always did.

She served the people faithfully, and soon many other servants came to join her in the work. Like her, they heard God's call and found their joy in serving others who could not pay them back. In time the world began to notice the work she was doing and they praised her. They built buildings for her work and gave money.

They honored her with awards. They felt better about themselves when they helped her. But she hardly noticed all of these things; they were unimportant to her. She only saw the endless needs of the people she served, and steadfastly pursued the mission that God had given her.

Years passed, and she continued to serve faithfully, even as osteoporosis bent her frail body. Because she kept her eyes on the hurting and dying in the streets she didn't seem to care that her physical condition rendered her unable to look anywhere but down. She also suffered many of the same maladies as the people she served because she lived among them and lived as they lived—on a meager diet in a filthy environment.[3]

Her face reflected the many hard years she had put in; the pain and hurt on the faces of those she served were mirrored on her own. But behind the wrinkled skin and tired eyes there was always love—love for those who were dying on the streets.

Unlike the princess, she did not offer a beautiful photo op. She looked frail and weak, as if a strong wind could blow her over. Yet she bravely withstood all of the hardships with amazing stamina. She stayed on, even when those around her urged her to take a break and leave the work to the younger and stronger ones.

She didn't take a break. And unlike the princess, she lived a long life. She was given a lot of time and she gave all of her time away to those in need.

She passed away peacefully, just as she had lived. One day she simply went to sleep and went to be with her Lord. Like the princess, she died with her lover, too. She was heard to say just before she left this life, "Jesus, I love you. Jesus, I love you."[4]

KING'S KIDS OR CHRIST'S SERVANTS?

The deaths of Princess Diana and Mother Teresa *within five days of each other* struck me as ironic. These were probably the best loved and most studied women of the world at that time. A beautiful young princess who would associate with the common people as she did charity work in her spare time made Diana the darling of the media.

Mother Teresa was also deeply admired, but she seemed a little too committed and selfless for most of us. It was hard to identify with her. Even reading about her life made me feel like a hypocrite. Here was someone who literally left all—her family, her homeland, her friends, and her possessions—to follow God's call. I often feel that I, like Diana, just dabble in good works while still protecting my space and my time.

The American church by and large wants to live as a princess. After all, we tell ourselves, we are the "King's Kids." We strut, we command, we decree, we take authority over demons and death. King's Kids walk with pride, not humility. We also grumble, complain, moan, nitpick, and nag when things don't go our way.

Because we belong to the King, we figure He should treat His kids better. I have often joked that if this is the way God treats His friends, I'd hate to be His enemy, implying that He is unjust and unfair in His treatment of me. I deserve better, I figure. After all, I am an heir of a royal priesthood and also a joint heir with the Son.

Am I a princess or a servant? It is true that I come from royal lineage; I am a child of God. But if God, my Creator, "made himself nothing, taking the very nature of a servant" (Philippians 2:7), then how can I think I deserve to live as royalty among so many that are oppressed and needy?

It was only after Christ was obedient to death that "God exalted him to the highest place and gave him the name that is above every name" (Philippians 2:9). And it is only after I am also willing to humble myself and become obedient to the death of my flesh, to spend myself "in behalf of the hungry and satisfy the needs of the oppressed," that I too will be exalted in my royal position. "Then your light will rise in the darkness" (Isaiah 58:10).

Much of the teaching in the church today revolves around our own needs and how to attain self-fulfillment. In the process of serving ourselves we have lost our voice in the community. People no longer trust preachers; they are very far down on the list of professions most admired in our society.

> **In the process of serving ourselves we have lost our voice in the community.**

And, sadly, few would see the church as the best place to go when they need help. We have witnessed the fall of many famous preachers. That is why my husband often says that he has more influence as a dentist than he does as a pastor.

What will it take to convince them that we can be trusted? Jesus is the King of Kings with a name so holy that "at the name of Jesus every knee should bow, in heaven and on earth and under the earth, and every tongue confess that Jesus Christ is Lord, to the glory of God the Father" (Philippians 2:10–11). Yet this One who had every reason to exalt himself did not flaunt his royal heritage when He walked the earth. Rather, He took on the form of a servant to give His life away for the good of others.

Claiming to be His followers, we must be careful how we conduct ourselves in the world. As His representatives we cannot expect to be treated as royalty if He was not. The apostle Peter knew that our status was for one purpose only—that we might glorify the awesome God who saved us. "You are a chosen people, a royal priesthood, a holy nation, a people belonging to God, *that you may declare the praises of him who called you out of darkness into his wonderful light*" (1 Peter 2:9).

How do we declare His praises? Jesus told us as He taught the crowds from the mountainside: "Let your light shine before men, that they may see your good deeds and praise your Father in heaven" (Matthew 5:16).

The Least of These: Our Litmus Test

Most of us recoil at the word *servant*. We do not want to be associated with the "least of these" but with the "movers and shakers" of the world. I certainly did not want to be associated with Mary Jane in my first grade class. She was the nerd of the class, the butt of all the little girls' jokes, and I joined in with my own ridicule.

One day I was in the cloak room passing out my birthday invitations. Suddenly there was a large shadow looming over me, and I looked up to see my teacher. "Do you have an invitation for Mary Jane?" she quietly asked me.

"Yes, I do, but I forgot it at home," I quickly lied.

"Well, don't forget to bring it tomorrow," she said firmly.

I was trapped. Mary Jane would ruin my party! She even smelled bad. But I had no choice—I couldn't face the displeasure of my teacher.

I can't remember many details about that party, except running down the stairs from my bedroom in my new patent leather shoes with all the little girls around me. I do remember how I felt—beautiful and loved. I always thought it was my new patent leather shoes that made me feel so wonderful.

It was years later, when God sent me to Brandon House to do ministry among "the least of these," that I realized why that moment at my birthday party has stayed with me so strongly. When I put aside my objections to her and reached out to Mary Jane, I enjoyed God's blessing on my party.

It is sad that it took me forty-two years to finally realize that the self-hatred I struggled with all my life could be healed by pouring myself out to "the least of these." When I am serving others in this way, I again feel beautiful and loved. I know I am pleasing my Father and that is my deepest desire.

Becoming God's Ground Force

In the same way, when we as the church serve the people of our communities under the inspiration of God's Spirit, we find joy as we fulfill our destiny and calling. It doesn't get any better than that! The fact that our impact is not dependent upon our size or wealth is especially exciting. We can make a difference for God no matter who we are or where we live, because our resource is God himself.

Jesus "did not come to be served, but to serve" (Matthew 20:28), and because "no servant is greater than his master" (John 13:16) we must do the same. We must willingly and obediently see ourselves as servants of the King.

As I mentioned in chapter 10, each individual church will express its servanthood in a unique way. But no matter whether our calling is in the area of worship, intercession (warriors), or working among the poor and needy, we are all part of God's team and we *can* win the battle. Together we can accomplish what is on God's heart—inviting everyone to His great banquet.

The parable of the great banquet, as recorded in Luke 14 and Matthew 22, makes the very strong point that we don't wait in our comfortable churches for people to come to us. We are called to *go out* to uncomfortable and scary places—streets, alleys, projects, inner cities, to the sick and disabled—and "bring," even "compel" them to come. God has moved beyond invitations; it is time for action.

Being God's ground force isn't easy. Not only are the surroundings "out there" sometimes out of our comfort zone and frightening, the reception we receive may also be disappointing. We must take the invitation to people who will be suspicious of our motives and often ungrateful and rude. We must continue to do the good works "which God prepared in advance for us to do" (Ephesians 2:10), serving and helping others till they finally see Christ in us.

We have much to overcome. We must dispel the wrong ideas about God and His church that have developed for all sorts of reasons. But we can begin to win their trust back by abandoning the role of "royalty" on earth and adopting the more biblical calling of serving those who need to know Him. It is not glamorous or pleasing to our flesh. But it is the path of joy and fulfillment.

At Spirit of God Fellowship we stumbled onto God's unique calling for us by letting the Holy Spirit lead us. We still do not trust in our own abilities but seek God in prayer for His will to be done in our church. We are ordinary people who carry an extraordinary invitation, and we are kept humble by failure and disappointment.

I know that nothing touches God's heart like unity among His people and a genuine concern for the poor and needy. Jesus chose Isaiah 61:1 for His inaugural sermon. He said that the Father anointed Him to preach to the poor and brokenhearted, to captives, prisoners, and all who mourn. These are the people who stand outside the walls of our churches, waiting for that precious invitation.

Hurricane Katrina in New Orleans brought Christians out of their comfort zone as they rushed to help those devastated by the storm. It also went a long way toward restoring confidence in not only the message but also the messengers. As a result, many Christians found that serving without any personal gain brought them into a new relationship with the Jesus of the Gospels, who also took the form of a servant.

I believe the church of Jesus is at that place in history Isaiah spoke about: "Arise, shine, for your light has come, and the glory of the Lord rises upon you" (Isaiah 60:1). It is time—we have learned more than we can ever live; we have worshiped, fasted, and interceded. Now is the time to step out of the familiar and risk, serve, love, and obey.

Taking God's invitation to those outside is all we're asked to do. The results are up to Him. "Let us not become weary in doing good, for at the proper time *we will reap a harvest if we do not give up*. Therefore, as we have opportunity, let us do good to all people" (Galatians 6:9–10).

Laying aside our royal robes as sons and daughters of the King of Kings, let us, like our Master, take "the very nature of a servant" and fulfill the Great Commission. Remember, it's the ground force that wins a decisive and lasting victory. The battle is hard; we experience defeats as well as victories; we grow weary and discouraged; we are challenged and elated. But oh . . . the rewards! To hear Him say, "Well done, good and faithful servant!" (Matthew 25:21) will be worth it all.

Come to the Party

Forgive me
for my grand missionary dreams
of sacrifice and dedication,
while ignoring the neighbor
you have placed on my doorstep.

Forgive me
for rejoicing in so great a salvation,
while friends and relatives
continue blindly on the road to hell.
Stop my mouth
from speaking out against injustice
while I promote by my lifestyle
that injustice daily.

Help me to live in reality
rather than escape to my fantasy world of idealism;
this allays my guilt,
but does nothing to further your kingdom.
Help me to leave the bright lights and
music of your party;
the secure intimacy of shared experience,
and seek those who stand
outside your love.

Keep me from being shocked by flesh unveiled,
as if my own flesh
were of a different substance.
Let me extend to them the hand
(your hand)
of love and acceptance.

Help me bring to your party,
those who have never known laughter
or music or dancing;
who knew somewhere there was a celebration,
but never dreamed
they would be invited!

Appendix

Restoration Ministries

Restoring People, Rebuilding Communities
253 E. 159th Street
Harvey, IL 60426
708–333–3370

Harvey House School of Ministry
253 E. 159th Street
Harvey, IL 60426
A residential Christian training facility for men who have overcome their addictions and/or criminal problems. This is an eighteen-month program where men with a desire to grow in Christ learn new life skills, rebuild broken relationships, and obtain job training. The men also assist in our other outreach ministries.

Tabitha House
15030 S. Dixie Highway
Harvey, IL 60426
A residential Christian training facility for women. The objective of this ministry is to provide an opportunity for a permanent life-changing experience to women who have overcome their addictions. In this eighteen-month program women complete their education, learn job skills, and rebuild relationships with their children.

Food Pantry

Harvey House

Mondays, 6:30 P.M.—8:00 P.M.

Our Food Pantry for residents of the city of Harvey is open every Monday night and provides food to more than four hundred families per month. Emergency food is given out as needed to community residents throughout the week as well. Restoration Ministries partners with the Greater Chicago Food Depository to supply the food products.

Restoration Ministries Thrift Stores

14950 Dixie Hwy. & 351 W. 162nd

South Holland, IL

Our thrift stores provide jobs and job training to community residents and Harvey House and Tabitha House residents. They sell good quality used clothing, furniture, household appliances, and other merchandise at low prices. Proceeds from the stores support Restoration Ministries' programs. In emergency cases, furniture, appliances, and clothing are donated to needy families.

Seniors Ministry

Harvey YMCA

Thursdays, 1:00—3:00 P.M.

Volunteers visit the seniors living at the Harvey YMCA for a weekly Bible study. In addition, volunteers are matched with seniors to provide the following for them: delivery of free food from our food pantry, rides to their doctors' appointments, social visits, and lots of love and companionship.

Seniors Banquet

Spirit of God Fellowship Hall

South Holland, IL

Twice a year, two hundred fifty senior citizens from the Harvey YMCA Senior Residence, the Robey Building (a senior public housing building), and community residents are treated to a banquet with all the trimmings. Dates for the banquets vary from year to year.

C.O.R.D.S. Prison Outreach

C.O.R.D.S., Christian Operation Restoration and Discipleship Safe House, is our prison ministry. A team of men travels to

Stateville Prison and Cook County Prison for Bible study and counseling. Upon their release from prison, men may enter the Harvey House School of Ministry.

Brandon House Outreach

This state-funded drug treatment facility has been a source of much of our ministry development. Volunteers and residents of Harvey House and Tabitha House conduct Bible studies, transport Brandon House residents to church services, and build relationships with them. Since the ministry began in 1982, nearly seven thousand individuals have had life-changing experiences to overcome their additions.

Overcomers Group

Harvey House

Fridays, 7:30 P.M.

A coed support group for recovering drug addicts, the Overcomers Group uses a Christian 12-Step program.

Fatherhood Initiative

Through this group the men of Harvey House are taught the importance of connecting with their children and methods for doing so effectively.

Block Party

Harvey House

Every summer (the date varies) Restoration Ministries holds a free block party for our neighbors. Free food, entertainment, a petting zoo, pony rides, games, and prizes are provided. Hundreds of families enjoy this outdoor event without fear of crime or violence.

The Christmas Toy Store

The Harvey Boxing Club

15331 Broadway

Harvey, IL

A unique way to provide toys to children from low-income families by making toys available to community residents at a minimal cost. Area schools, churches, and businesses collect and donate brand-new toys that are sold at our annual Toy Store. Toys are priced between $1.00 and $5.00.

Salvation Army Extension Site

Restoration Ministries serves as the Salvation Army site for Harvey residents. Upon the Salvation Army's request, Restoration Ministries' staff distribute Salvation Army's emergency and general assistance funds to Harvey residents.

Operation Crossover

Suburban congregations and inner-city churches partner together to work with Restoration Ministries to change neighborhoods and serve those in need.

Oak Forest Hospital Ministry

Volunteers and residents of Harvey House visit patients suffering from long-term illnesses at this county hospital every week. For some of these patients, our volunteers are the only visitors they get. The volunteers pray with the patients as well as take care of their personal needs, such as giving them haircuts, bringing them snacks, and giving them Bibles and other gifts.

Inner City Interns

This program was established to share our success in ministering to the inner-city environment. Young adults from around the United States come to Restoration Ministries for hands-on training in working with urban outreaches.

Restoration Ministries' Project Intercept Gang Prevention Program

"Train a child in the way he should go,
and when he is old he will not turn from it"
(Proverbs 22:6).

The Harvey Boxing Club

15331 Broadway
Harvey, IL
Monday—Saturday, 708–333–8353

The Harvey Boxing Club gives boys and girls an opportunity to be trained by professional trainers and coaches in the sport of boxing. Boxing requires discipline and self-motivation and is a proven delinquency deterrent. The Boxing Club won the 2005 Illinois State Silver Gloves Team Title.

Gallery of The Arts

15331 Broadway

Harvey, IL

Monday—Saturday

Our Arts Education Program provides underprivileged children and teens high-quality visual and performing arts classes. Classes are taught by professional artists and teachers. Our goal is to nurture the talents of young people and channel their energy into the creation and celebration of art.

Kids Café

Harvey House

Monday—Friday, 3:00—4:00 P.M.

Restoration Ministries, in partnership with the Greater Chicago Food Depository and Second Harvest, is a site for a Kids Café. Through the Kids Café we provide hot, nutritious meals every day after school to children and teens.

Tutoring and Homework Help

Harvey House

Monday—Friday, 3:30—5:00 P.M.

Elementary and junior-high students get help with their homework and special projects through this program. They are tutored after school by the director of Project Intercept, who is a teacher.

Kids Computer Club

Harvey House

Mondays, Tuesdays, and Thursdays, 3:30—5:00 P.M.

Here children learn the fundamentals of computer usage and use the computers on site to complete homework and projects. This program provides children from low-income families access to computers.

Academic Enrichment

Through this program we take the children who participate in our tutoring program and Computer Club on field trips and special outings.

Summer Day Camp

Harvey House

(dates vary)

Our annual day camp, based on the Say YES (Save America's Youth) program, helps kids develop spiritually, physically, morally, and intellectually. Attendees have lunch, play games, do activities (arts and crafts, etc.), and go on field trips. Each week has a theme based on a Bible verse.

Vacation Bible School

Harvey House

(dates vary each year)

More than one hundred twenty kids participate in our annual weeklong camp of Bible study, games, lunch, and fun.

Hoops 'n Rap

Boys meet at Harvey House

Fridays, 7:00—10:00 P.M.

Hoops 'n Rap is a basketball program that meets weekly for open gym at a local school. Every Friday night, year-round, more than seventy-five boys between the ages of thirteen and nineteen come to play basketball together. Each night begins with a fifteen-minute rap session, where the teenagers are given a chance to share their struggles, concerns, and experiences, and seek counsel from the director of the program and the coaches. In addition to open gym, basketball teams are formed that compete in various basketball leagues and tournaments throughout the Chicago area.

Brooks Junior High School Outreach

Tuesdays

Residents of Harvey House and Tabitha House go to Brooks once a week as mentors to reach out to the students and develop friendships with them during their lunch periods.

Brooks Junior High Spring Break Camp

(dates vary each year)

During Spring Break Restoration Ministries takes one hundred elementary and junior high students to Silver Birch Ranch in White Lake, Wisconsin. During this annual trip, kids hear a clear presentation of the gospel and participate in workshops on topics that affect their lives back home—drugs, gangs, and abstinence. They also ride horses, raft, play games, and have a lot of fun.

Summer Camp

Restoration Ministries offers children an opportunity to attend weeklong Christian camps in Wisconsin, Missouri, and Indiana. In addition to providing fun and challenging activities, including swimming, fishing, hiking, sports, and arts and crafts, all the camps have a spiritual focus.

Thornton High School Outreach

Our executive director serves as chaplain for the Thornton High School football team. He also mentors students at Thornton High School.

Youth Group

Tuesday Nights, 7:30—9:00 P.M.
Youth Building on Spirit of God Campus
16400 State
South Holland, IL

Eighty-five junior high and high school students from different cultural and socioeconomic backgrounds meet every Tuesday night for worship, biblical teaching, games, and life lessons that pertain to their everyday lives. Topics include submitting to authority, abstinence, and giving back to the community.

Learn More About Restoration Ministries

Restoring People, Rebuilding Communities

Barbara and John Sullivan founded Restoration Ministries in 1988 to minister the gospel and love of Jesus Christ to poor, disenfranchised, and hurting people. Their desire was to touch the inner city with programs that would facilitate permanent change in the lives of those living in economic, spiritual, and physical poverty. The mission of Restoration Ministries is to impact lives in ways that will restore hope to people while bringing change to their community.

Today Restoration Ministries operates thirty programs. With the help of more than four hundred and fifty dedicated volunteers, it is able to serve seven thousand individuals annually through its programs. Reaching out to all segments of the population, it has become a beacon of hope for families, senior citizens, ex-criminals, recovering drug addicts, and at-risk, underprivileged youth.

For more information on Restoration Ministries, including arranging a tour of the facilities or details on volunteer and giving opportunities, go to its Web site: *restorationministries.net* or call: 708–333–3370.

Author Information

In addition to Restoration Ministries, Barbara and John Sullivan pioneered together a nondenominational church in South Holland, Illinois, called Spirit of God Fellowship, which now includes a Christian grammar school. Barbara is a graduate of Loyola University of Chicago and has authored four books, including *The Control Trap*, published by Bethany House Publishers.

Barbara has made appearances on numerous radio and TV shows that include the 700 Club (U.S.A.) and 100 Huntley Street (Canada). She has spoken at many women's ministry events throughout the country sponsored by local churches, Christian Women's Clubs, and MOPS groups. In her own area she regularly teaches Bible studies to recovering addicts at a state drug rehab center, as well as speaks to Christian groups on ministry to the needy.

Barbara can be contacted by e-mail: barbsully@comcast.net, or through the Web site: *restorationministries.net*.

Endnotes

Introduction

1. George Barna, *The Second Coming of the Church* (Nashville: Word Publishing, 1998), 1.
2. Paul Tournier, *The Adventure of Living* (New York: Harper & Row, 1965), 149–50.
3. Barna Research Online, "Small Churches Struggle to Grow Because of the People They Attract" (September 2, 2003), *www.barna.org.*

Chapter 2

1. Richard Daigle, "Escape From the Suburbs," *Charisma*, May 2003, 68–74.
2. W. E. Vine, *An Expository Dictionary of New Testament Words* (Westwood, NJ: Fleming H. Revell Company, 1966), 181.

Chapter 3

1. Adrienne S. Gaines, "Campus Crusade for Christ Founder, Bill Bright, Dies," *Charisma*, September 2003, 15.
2. George Barna, *The Second Coming of the Church*, 3.

Chapter 4

1. Charles Colson, *Being the Body* (Nashville: Word Publishing Group, 2003), 207.
2. George Barna, *The Second Coming of the Church*, 33, emphasis added.
3. Ibid., 36.
4. Ibid., 34.

Chapter 5

1. George Barna, *The Second Coming of the Church*, 18.
2. Jay E. Adams, *Competent to Counsel* (Grand Rapids, MI: Zondervan, 1970), 41.
3. Ibid.
4. Ibid.
5. Karl Olsson, *Come to the Party* (Waco, TX: Word Incorporated, 1972), 98.
6. Ibid., 126.
7. Charles Colson, *Being the Body*, 107.
8. D. Michael Henderson, *John Wesley's Class Meeting* (Nappanee, IN: Evangel Publishing House, 1997), 14.
9. Ibid., 28.
10. Ibid., 121.

Chapter 6

1. Ron Luce, "Running From God," *Charisma*, September 2005, 38.

Chapter 7

1. John Dawson, *Taking Our Cities for God* (Lake Mary, FL: Charisma House, 1990).

Chapter 8

1. Eileen Egan and Kathleen Egan, OSB, *Suffering Into Joy* (Ann Arbor, MI: Servant Publications, 1994), 48.

Chapter 9

1. Charles Simpson, "Circle or Vine?" *A Pastoral Letter From Charles Simpson* (May 2003), 1–4, emphasis added.
2. Ibid., 3, emphasis added.
3. Ibid.
4. George Barna, *The Second Coming of the Church*, 18.
5. D. Michael Henderson, *John Wesley's Class Meeting*, 26.

Chapter 10

1. Phillip Keller, *A Shepherd Looks at Psalm 23* (Grand Rapids, MI: Daybreak Books, 1970), 40.

Chapter 11

1. Donna Jackson Nakazawa, "The Changing Faces of America," *Chicago Tribune, Parade Magazine* (July 6, 2003), 4.
2. Arnold Mulder, *Americans From Holland* (New York: J. B. Lippincott Company, 1947), 143.

Chapter 12

1. V. Dion Haynes, "Hunger has a new face," *Chicago Tribune*, Section 1, Nation, September 1, 2003, 10.
2. D. Michael Henderson, *John Wesley's Class Meeting*, 28.
3. Charles Colson, *Being the Body*, 269.
4. Charles Haddon Spurgeon, *The Gospel of Matthew* (Grand Rapids, MI: Fleming H. Revell, 1987), 372.

Chapter 13

1. Rod Nordland, *Newsweek* (October 29, 1997), 35.
2. Eileen Egan and Kathleen Egan, OSB, *Suffering Into Joy*, 65.
3. Lucinda Vardey, comp., *Mother Teresa, A Simple Path* (New York: Ballantine Books, 1995), xix.
4. Mother Teresa, *Famous Last Words*, September 5, 1997, *Worldvillage.com*.